# EVEN
# WHEN

Sara Pasterski
Psalm 117

# EVEN WHEN

---

Rejoicing in God's Faithfulness through
Life's Uncertainty, Disappointment, and Loss

## SARA PASTERSKI

First paperback edition August 2019

Cover design by Sara Pasterski
Cover photography by Timothy M. Sailer

ISBN 978-1-0821-9450-4 (paperback)

For more information:
*authorsarapasterski@outlook.com*
*facebook.com/authorsarapasterski*

*For my Creator, Sustainer, Redeemer, and Savior, the one true God. May the words on these pages go forth to bring glory and honor and praise to Your name alone.*

*Grace was mine, glory is His.*

# WITH GRATEFUL THANKS

To Peter, my beloved husband, who has loved and supported me through all that the marriage of two sinners entails, and for blessing me with the great privilege of working in the home.

To Pastor Brian Marchi, who selflessly gave of his time to read this manuscript and use his gifts entrusted by God to ensure a biblically-sound book.

To all my sisters in Christ in Wisconsin, Tennessee, and Florida, who faithfully prayed through this whole process of writing, that the result may be to God's glory.

To the pastors mentioned in this book, through whom I have learned so much about our beloved God, matured under their preaching, and been influenced greatly by their life examples.

To Lorrie Blaylock, who encouraged, supported, and offered practical help from the beginning of this endeavor.

To Tom Loomer, my genuine and caring stepfather, for applying your God-given gifts to help me communicate most effectively.

To my mom, who has always been my greatest cheerleader and encourager, and for each of the ways you contributed to this book.

To Diane Stroobants, for giving me the perfect idea for this book's main title.

# CONTENTS

# INTRODUCTION

I believe that God was stirring in my heart for over a decade to write a book. I never knew exactly what the book's theme would be, but I had a general idea. When looking at a bird's eye view of over four decades traveling around the sun, I could perceive that several life circumstances had been sovereignly and lovingly ordained by God in my life that were not as typical in others' lives. It's not that the circumstances were the subject to write about, but rather how God had brought me to the surface from these various trials with a stronger trust in Him. I've experienced a contentment that was not the result of the stereotypical and predictable happily-ever-after ending that sometimes concludes books about hope, faith, and trust.

Though the endeavor of writing a book had been on my heart for more than 10 years, I believe it's not something that one ought to rush into. The Lord drew my heart to Himself in saving faith in 1998, and while enthusiasm and zeal for the Lord consumed me, wisdom, spiritual maturity, and seasons of sanctification had not yet penetrated my profusely prideful existence! I can laugh in wholehearted agreement as modern hymn-writer Keith Getty quoted Pastor Alistair Begg's response to his idea of writing a book earlier in his life,

> *"If you write a book before you're 40, I personally will break your legs with a baseball bat."*[1]

I cringe at so many things I arrogantly and ignorantly said and did as a young believer - who am I kidding, I cringe at things I just said yesterday. But as a young believer I was completely clueless on sound doctrine and proper hermeneutics to study God's Word. There is much personal growth that ought to occur as a student of the Word diligently mines God's Word to behold Him, to know Him more fully year after year (2 Corinthians 3:18), in conjunction with the discipline that the Lord brings upon those He loves (Hebrews 12:6-11) to conform them to His image (Romans 8:29).

Coupled with personal growth and sanctification over two decades, the Lord generously led me to opportunities to begin understanding how to study His Word properly through participation in several biblical exposition workshops for women teaching women. Now having some cognitively practical tools to study the Word, and having received pastoral affirmation of a writing gift, I trust the Lord was building one block upon another to prepare me for this season of writing professionally.

A strong desire of my heart is to grow into a Titus 2 older woman. I praise God for the discipline He's taken me through continuously over 20 years (and counting!) to refine me, grow me doctrinally, and change sinful patterns that had previously disqualified me completely from this noble title of an older woman. I love mentoring younger women through impromptu conversations where I may be allowed to speak God-honoring wisdom into similar situations I've experienced in 19 years of marriage and 21 years' life experience under my Shepherd's guidance.

Through personal prayers and those of faithful friends, the timing became evident that I should begin this book project. God provided me with a resource that showed me how to map out the myriad ideas swimming in my head, and, from this exercise, the theme of God's faithfulness clearly emerged.

The purpose of this book is twofold: to glorify God and to bless and benefit others. I desire to bring forth a book, particularly for women, that recognizes and honors God's faithfulness and His sovereignty, and is saturated with His Truth for a world that is overflowing with humanistic and superficial counterfeits. May the time you spend reading these pages invoke a higher view of God, yield an increased trust in Him, and inspire hope through Christ alone.

Soli Deo Gloria

# CHAPTER ONE

# WHAT IS FAITHFULNESS?

*"Great is Thy Faithfulness, O God my Father"[1]*

"Great is Thy Faithfulness" is my all-time favorite hymn. I doubt there is a reader holding this book who hasn't sung it or at least heard of it. While many of us may have grown up singing this song and may sing it to this day, who has paused to reflect on what the word faithful means, particularly in the context of describing our great God as faithful?

Faithfulness is defined as having a strict adherence to truth or to a promise or vow. God is the only One in our lives who is perfectly faithful. He is divine. We are so completely unlike Him in our sinfulness and imperfections that we can never be perfectly faithful, try as we might. Numbers 23:19 tells us:

> *"God is not a man, that He should lie,*
> *Nor a son of man, that He should repent;*
> *Has He said, and will He not do it?*
> *Or has He spoken, and will He not do it?"*

Simply stated, by describing God as faithful, it means that God will always do what He has said, and He will fulfill all His promises.

I recently heard the question posed, "Is there anything God cannot do?" An impulsive response, my own included, may seem to answer that question, "Of course not! God can do anything!" But a thoughtful examination of the question, however, results in the answer resembling the truth that "God cannot do anything contrary to His nature." If God could be unfaithful to who He has declared Himself to be in Scripture, then He would not be the perfect, holy, righteous, and unblemished God that He is (Deuteronomy 32:4).

Another skewed belief many of us may embrace is that God is faithful *if* things work out well for us. We may believe that God's faithfulness is justified only by happily-ever-after circumstances and prayers answered in the specific way we prayed for something. God is faithful not only when all seems well with us, but He is most definitely faithful when we face trials. This is a vital truth we must understand in our adversities and in the darkness of circumstances we're facing. Psalm 73:26 reminds us:

> *My flesh and my heart may fail,*
> *But God is the strength of my heart and my portion*
> *forever.*

God's Word is full of truth and promises we can cling to through every season of life. Knowing He is faithful to keep His word is what we base this assurance on.

> *For the word of the LORD is upright,*
> *And all His work is done in faithfulness.*
> PSALM 33:4

## FAMILIAR UNFAITHFULNESS

All people, believers or not, will fail us and will be unfaithful toward us in one way or another. When you pause to think about it, it happens all the time. Just this morning while writing this book during a season of navigating a health issue, I had an instance of someone's unfaithfulness occur. A doctor told me he would get back to me with the results from my lab-work yesterday, but didn't get back to me until today. No one, including me, is faultless in this struggle. Also just this morning I set up plans with a friend to meet the following

Monday. Yet minutes later I was changing my commitment after realizing I already had an appointment.

Of course these are such minor and rather painless examples. We could all likely recount deeply painful instances of unfaithfulness we've seen or experienced in personal relationships, and we'd describe the ravages this sin brings upon families. My trite examples are simply to show how prevalent faithfulness and unfaithfulness are in our everyday lives. Why can't we just do what we say we'll do, or be who we say we are? To quote Pastor Matt Stanchek, "You're a lump of clay that's been animated by God for a brief season, and a sinful one at that."[2]

These examples are so everyday commonplace that we may not even think about how unfaithful we truly are as God's mere creatures. I'm going to believe that the doctor I shared about was not malicious at all in his intent, nor was I in creating a plan with my friend. Rather as sinful, fallen man, we cannot help ourselves from failing one another from time to time, at best, but realistically we fail one another daily!

We give ourselves far more credit than we deserve. As God states in Psalm 50:21, "You thought that I was altogether like you". It commonly plagues us as believers to embrace far too low a view of God, and far, *far* too high a view of ourselves. Who cannot use the constant reminder that we are utterly unlike the God Most High?

*Who is like the LORD our God,*
*Who is enthroned on high,*
*Who humbles Himself to behold*
*The things that are in heaven and in the earth?*
PSALM 113:5-6

When given a closer examination, we will see even more clearly how unfaithful we are in the shadow of the Almighty.

## One who is Faithful & True

A very valuable use of time for believers would be studying and reflecting more often on God's attributes. His attributes include His self-existence, sovereignty, omnipresence , omnipotence, eternality, immutability/unchangeableness, His love, knowledge, mercy, justice, holiness, and faithfulness, to name a few. This worthwhile study and reflection ought to invoke awe and worship of God for who He is. The time spent would also help us recognize how we fall so inadequately short and are nothing without Him. We owe any goodness about ourselves to His Holy Spirit inside us.

To declare God faithful, we are also affirming that all His words are true and are the final standard of truth. There is no book that is equal. In a society where truth is commonly touted as relative, and many times defined by one's personal desires or bents toward sin, God's timeless words remain the final standard of truth (John 17:17, 2 Timothy 3:16).

*The sum of Your word is truth,*
*And every one of Your righteous ordinances is everlasting.*
Psalm 119:160

In our daily lives we hear a variety of voices, whether audibly or through cultural influence, that vie for our affections, our attention, and our allegiance. The voices of the world are selling us lies, selling us their products that cannot deliver on their empty promises for fulfillment and significance. They're selling us false hope that contentment and joy is just around the corner after we do, buy, or experience "XYZ". They are utterly unfaithful to deliver the true joy our hearts are hungry for.

In my vapor-like existence to-date, I can testify that the absolutely most fulfilling and richest times of communion, contentment, and fellowship are when my eyes are undistractedly on my Savior, and I am deep into His truths on the pages of scripture. It feels like an other-worldly experience, because it is; God's Word is

9

the bedrock of all truth and purity that we can get our hands upon and our hearts wrapped around in this temporary, unfulfilling world.

Regarding every promise in the Bible, we can fully depend on God to do what He has said He'll do. He is worthy to be relied upon and will be faithful to fulfill all He's promised. As Deuteronomy 7:9 declares,

> *Know therefore that the LORD your God, He is God, the faithful God, who keeps His covenant and His lovingkindness to a thousandth generation with those who love Him and keep His commandments.*

If you're also a believer, you emphatically agree that God's Word is truth, and He is worthy to be trusted, and only He will satisfy our deepest longings. But our lives can oftentimes reflect the opposite of that truth, and we try to take matters into our own hands. We doubt the faithfulness of God's word by our sinful worry over any concern. We undermine His authority by following any given path that feels good and seems right in our own eyes. We show distrust of His sovereignty when we disobediently grumble or even work to orchestrate events to suit our selfish desires and comforts, rather than submitting obediently and trusting His control over the circumstance. We drown out His voice of truth when we allow the world's opinions to seep into our thinking, and we take on a pragmatic approach when things seem right if they're working well. We dismiss God as insufficient when we settle for cheap substitutes, grasping for temporary fulfillment and pseudo-satisfaction.

As we press on through each chapter of this book, we'll dig more deeply into how God shows Himself faithful in our lives through examples from various biblical accounts, and historical and personal examples. Oh, that we'd take God at His word and not need supplemental reminders to point us back to the Author and Perfecter of our faith (Hebrews 12:2), but thanks be to God that He uses us to display His powerful works to a watching and hurting world (John 9:3).

QUESTIONS FOR REFLECTION

1. What is the definition of faithfulness (page 6)?

2. Psalm 50:21 confronts us with the truth, "You thought that I was altogether like you". Read Psalm 113:5-6. In what ways do you find yourself holding a lower view of God than He is worthy of? Reflect on whether there are ways you treat Him as you would treat a good friend, as an equal.

3. According to Deuteronomy 7:9, who does God keep His commandments with?

4. God is faithful and His Word is true. Reflect on ways in which you regularly allow the voices of the world to usurp God's truth in your life.

## CHAPTER TWO

# WHEN TRIALS COME

*Consider it all joy, my brethren,*
*when you encounter various trials*
JAMES 1:2

Do you have blissful memories of carefree days and years as a child, where your biggest concern for the day was what to play next or how you'd have the most fun indoors if the weather did not permit outdoor adventures that day? I know this is certainly not the case for all holding this book, but for many readers I hope you can recall with fondness a virtually obligation-free existence that's typically characterized by childhood. Swimming, biking, building forts, playing sports, birthday parties, sticky popsicle fingers, perhaps a family vacation now and then; the list of simple pleasures could go on and on. Though it may have been enjoyable, would it be beneficial for us to continue through all of life in that fashion?

We may have been free from "adult-size" trials and cares that come along with adulthood responsibilities, but in that context we could also be largely denied the depth of growth and refinement that trials produce. We can be certain that there is much to refine in each of us, beginning in our childhood. Proverbs 22:15 confirms for us that foolishness is bound up in the heart of a child. We were blessed if we had parents who didn't thwart trials from our path, parents who used a rod of discipline to help us learn age-appropriate lessons to the glory of God.

I don't have to illustrate to you that life gets more complicated and stressful as we age. Adult-size trials bring upon us more angst and bigger consequences than having a favorite toy taken away. Let's look at the beauty of these God-ordained trials and how we can look upon them as beneficial blessings.

This chapter's title was inspired by The Gettys' song[1] of the same name. Its opening lyrics declare,

> *When trials come no longer fear*
> *For in the pain our God draws near*
> *To fire a faith worth more than gold*
> *And there His faithfulness is told*
> *And there His faithfulness is told*

The Lord has shown us in His Word several reasons that trials occur in our lives. He is God and He is sovereign. We can absolutely trust that He purposes to accomplish the cultivation of these beneficial attributes He's promised us.

> *And not only this, but we also exult in our tribulations, knowing that tribulation brings about perseverance; and perseverance, proven character, and proven character, hope; and hope does not disappoint, because the love of God has been poured out within our hearts through the Holy Spirit who was given to us.*
> ROMANS 5:3-5

> *Consider it all joy, my brethren, when you encounter various trials, knowing that the testing of your faith produces endurance. And let endurance have its perfect result, so that you may be perfect and complete, lacking in nothing.*
> JAMES 1:2-3

Certainly there are more verses about trials, such as 1 Peter 1:6-7, 4:12-13, 5:10; 2 Corinthians 4:8-10, 17; 2 Corinthians 12:10; 2 Timothy 3:12, and Matthew 5:10-12. But the context in which I'm focusing on this chapter is most pertinent under the umbrella of Romans 5:3-5 and James 1:2-3.

## ETYMOLOGY

Let's begin by breaking down Romans 5:3-5 in its original context and language to ensure we're working from an accurate interpretation. At a very high-level-view, the book of Romans contains the apostle Paul's letter to the believers in Rome, describing the unrighteousness of mankind, followed by an examination of the gospel with its undeniable ramifications.

Paul opens the fifth chapter of this theological masterpiece by affirming justification by faith and the resulting peace with God through our Lord Jesus Christ (Romans 5:1). He continues that we stand in this grace because Christ has brought us to this position, and we rejoice in the hope that we have a glorious future in God's presence (Romans 5:2).

This context sets us up to continue examining verses 3-5. Paul proceeds, writing, *"And not only this, but we also exult in our tribulations"*. So, not only do we celebrate the hope we have in a glorious future in God's presence because of Jesus Christ's payment of our debt, making us guiltless and righteous before a holy God (justification), but Paul says we are also to celebrate in our tribulations. The original word here for tribulations means a pressing, or pressure, anything which burdens the spirit. It is sometimes coupled with anguish, distress, persecution, and to suffer affliction due to the pressure of circumstances[2].

We can easily understand how the opening verses of Romans 5 are cause for celebration, as the gospel is unequivocally the best news ever, but what is Paul getting at by stating that we exult in our tribulations?

15

Paul continues, *"knowing that tribulation brings about perseverance; and perseverance, proven character, and proven character, hope"*. Tribulation - our afflictions, our distresses, that which we suffer - brings about perseverance, which is *a remaining under* in the Greek. Remaining under, or possessing a patient endurance or steadfastness, brings about proven character, and proven character, hope.

How often do we take a magnifying glass approach to our distressing circumstances? It's so natural and easy to have blinders on to seeing that there is a bigger purpose happening than what's right in front of our eyes.

Do you get tunnel-vision, like me, and find it laborious to lift your eyes upward from your horizontal perspective on this temporary, spherical residence we're living upon? But the apostle Paul declares that we boast, or glory, in our troubles. Yes, everything we go through God is using for our good and His glory (Romans 8:28-30), not that it may *feel* good, but it's *for* our good.

Likewise, James affirms that we ought to *"consider it all joy"* when we *"encounter various trials"*! But why? He continues, *"knowing that the testing of your faith produces endurance. And let endurance have its perfect result, so that you may be perfect and complete, lacking in nothing."*

James is teaching us the same thing Paul is teaching us in Romans 5, that trials produce perseverance and patient endurance. Such God-ordained occurrences in our lives are used to bring us into greater maturity (perfect and complete) each time we remain under a trial.

## PATIENT ENDURANCE SHOWN IN THE WORD

The first virtue that Paul lists as a fruit of our affliction is perseverance, or a steadfast endurance under a trial. In addition to growing in maturity and patient endurance, James describes believers who successfully endure trials as truly happy. He affirms that as a result of their genuine and enduring faith they will have the ultimate reward of eternal life.

> *Blessed is a man who perseveres under trial; for once he has been approved, he will receive the crown of life which the Lord has promised to those who love Him.*
> JAMES 1:12

Are you prone to grumble at the first sign of a trial in your life? All too often I know I am. It's imperative to bow our lives, our wills, before our Sovereign God and elevate our eyes from the distressing details we're so easily caught up in. How many missed opportunities are we squandering that we could be focusing on and elevating our affections to the God Most High through His building of our trust and enduring patience in His sovereignty over our circumstances.

It's in the trials that require perseverance that we can become impatient, even demanding of God our way in our time. Or, by living contrary to having impatience, we can grow exponentially in our trust in and reliance on Him.

During the waiting we are also prone to sinful worry, as opposed to releasing our imagined control and relying on the One who holds the world in His hand (Psalm 95:4-5). I can only write about this because I've struggled and continue to battle, at times, with this adversary called anxiousness and impatience.

How can we endure in our afflictions? We can't…on our own, in our strength (2 Corinthians 12:9-10). God will take care of our hearts; however, we must repent of our sinful anxiety and go to Him in prayer. Obediently yielding to and applying the truth in Philippians 4:6-8 is a tremendous start.

> *Be anxious for nothing, but in everything by prayer and supplication with thanksgiving let your requests be made known to God.*

*And the peace of God, which surpasses all comprehension, will guard your hearts and minds in Christ Jesus.*

*Finally, brethren, whatever is true, whatever is honorable, whatever is right, whatever is pure, whatever is lovely, whatever is of good repute, if there is any excellence and if anything worth of praise, dwell on these things.*

PHILIPPIANS 4:6-8

By God's grace alone He works in our hearts to cultivate enduring patience in and with the tribulation. Bible commentator Matthew Henry stated this concept beautifully:

"THAT WHICH WORKETH PATIENCE IS MATTER OF JOY; FOR PATIENCE DOES US MORE GOOD THAN TRIBULATIONS CAN DO US HURT. TRIBULATION IN ITSELF WORKETH IMPATIENCE; BUT, AS IT IS SANCTIFIED TO THE SAINTS, IT WORKETH PATIENCE."[3]

When considering biblical accounts of afflictions, we can certainly think of Job right away. He was a man in whom God cultivated an enduring patience, albeit an imperfect one in the process (Job 21:4), and whose character and devotion to God were proven through great affliction in the loss of all his children, livestock, and servants. God described Job as a blameless and upright man (Job 1:8), and after the initial, extensive devastation that God allowed Satan to unleash in Job's life, Job blessed the name of the LORD (Job 1:21) and God approved Job's character as he held fast his integrity (Job 2:3).

Likewise, how much enduring patience and perseverance did Joseph demonstrate in Genesis 37-50. He was sold into slavery by his brothers and later thrown in prison over false accusations by his boss' wife, all the while being separated from the father he loved.

God vindicates Joseph's faithfulness, puts him in an honorable position of high leadership, and uses Joseph to bless the nations by providing grain during a severe famine, first for Egypt (Genesis 41:56) then for all the earth (Genesis 41:57). Joseph's is a marvelous account of God's providence, of glory through suffering.

## STEADFASTNESS SHOWN IN OUR GENERATION

Let us consider now the enduring patience and perseverance of someone from our own lifetime. I'd be remiss to write a chapter on trials and not include one of my favorite sisters in Christ from days gone by.

Apart from the people we know in the Bible, Corrie ten Boom is the one person from history that I'd most delight in having a dialogue with. Her book, *The Hiding Place*[4] is one of the most life-changing books I've read aside from the Bible. Corrie and her family were holocaust heroes. They helped save the lives of over 800 Jews during World War II in Holland. At the risk of their own lives, this remarkable family continually hid people behind a wall in their home. Though these selfless, sacrificial acts to help save so many people were astonishingly admirable, it was their subsequent life in the Nazi concentration camps that most deeply permeated the prideful, discontent, idolatrous layers of my own heart.

One of the most awe-inspiring examples set by Corrie and her sister Betsie in Ravensbruck concentration camp was their handling of the fleas in their barracks. While laying on soiled-straw-covered platform "beds", they discovered their meager surroundings were swarming with fleas. In desperation, Corrie wailed to her sister, asking how they could live in such a place. God faithfully answered Betsie's cry, asking Him to show them how, by leading them to 1 Thessalonians 5:14-18, which concludes with "in everything give thanks; for this is God's will for you in Christ Jesus." A skeptical Corrie requested an example of what they could possibly give thanks for, and Betsie reminded her of the enormous blessing it was that they were assigned to be together in the camp. Betsie continued with

19

reminding Corrie of the fact that they held a Bible in their hands; God had miraculously allowed them to sneak a forbidden Bible into the death camp.

They continued to thank God for the crowding of the barracks, that more may hear the Word of God through them. When Betsie offered up a prayer of thanksgiving for the fleas, Corrie thought that was a bit too much! With disbelief she declared that there was no way even God could make her grateful for a flea. Betsie reminded Corrie that God's Word says in *everything* give thanks, not just pleasant circumstances, and that fleas were part of where God had put them.

As days passed, the sisters took notice of the fact that the guards were very minimally patrolling their barracks, often not wanting to step foot inside, and this gave Betsie and Corrie the opportunity to share their faith and read from the Bible to the many women around them. They were offering two Bible studies a night, worshipping God in the most deplorable conditions imaginable. The faithful women later found the reason the guards would rarely set foot in their barracks was because it was so infested with fleas! Corrie then humbly recalled with reverence her sister's emphatic enlightenment of 1 Thessalonians 5:18, in everything give thanks; for this is God's will for you in Christ Jesus.

Reading that book stirred a conviction within me to consider how, far too often, I am not giving thanks to God in everything. Likewise, it incited me to consistently examine the prevalent discontentment I allow to propagate in my heart. The ten Boom sisters' model of humble gratitude is one I ought to read and recall to memory on a regular basis. I cannot more highly recommend your reading of *The Hiding Place* and Corrie's later book *Tramp for the Lord.*

Betsie and Corrie ten Boom are incredible testaments to lives lived in full and complete trust in God, persevering by His grace and strength in the worst of earthly circumstances. These sisters' glorification of God rings through in two quotes from *The Hiding*

*Place* that you may have heard before, but will certainly generate more hope from.

> "THERE IS NO PIT SO DEEP
> THAT HE IS NOT DEEPER STILL."
> *Betsie ten Boom*

> "JOY RUNS DEEPER THAN DESPAIR"
> *Corrie ten Boom*

Believers who face affliction, by the grace of God, develop perseverance. A believer who has endured affliction will develop character. The experiences that God sovereignly allowed in in the lives of Job, Joseph, and Betsie and Corrie ten Boom undoubtedly cultivated their character, and ultimately manifested in hope, as promised in our focal verse Romans 5:3-5.

## PROVEN CHARACTER

Reflecting back on Romans 5:4, Paul secondly lists *proven character* as a result of the enduring patience and perseverance God cultivates in us through afflictions. The Greek for this phrase is *the process of proving* and is rendered experience.

God builds steadfastness and perseverance in us through the afflictions we go through, and these experiences ought to increasingly amplify our trust in Him for our next incident or season of difficulties. No two trials are exactly identical, but as we allow God to build one experiential "block" upon another, we find ourselves standing as a "fortress" of unshakeable faith and trust through His strength and faithfulness. Each small trial increases our trust and aids us in proving a faithful, godly character in the bigger trials.

Proven godly character can be characterized by many attributes such as love, joy, peace, patience, kindness, goodness, faithfulness, gentleness, self-control, purity, compassion, humility,

21

meekness, a forgiving spirit, and contentment (Galatians 5:22-23; Colossians 3:12-15).

Possessing true contentment is certainly a mark of proven character. When we exhibit discontentment, we are denying that God is the sovereign God that He is, and we are not trusting His goodness and faithfulness. Essentially, we are denying what we claim to believe about God. We are believing a lie that we're entitled to something we perceive as better, and that God is allowing this supposed injustice.

Paul and Timothy teach us about the growth that occurs through learning contentment. As they write in Philippians 4:11-13,

> *11Not that I speak from want, for I have learned to be content in whatever circumstances I am. 12I know how to get along with humble means, and I also know how to live in prosperity; in any and every circumstance I have learned the secret of being filled and going hungry, both of having abundance and suffering need. 13I can do all things through Him who strengthens me.*

Similarly, Paul writes to Timothy in 1 Timothy 6:6,

> *But godliness actually is a means of great gain when accompanied by contentment.*

The context of contentment that Paul spoke from in these verses was far from pleasant or free from afflictions. In fact, the majority of us cannot even come close to relating to Paul's life experiences in the ministry. Paul spent years of his life in prison. Paul remained faithful in trusting God through deplorable, miserable, and cold imprisonments, hunger and thirst, beatings, stoning, regularly in dangerous situations, and overnight in the deep from a shipwreck at sea (2 Corinthians 11:23-27). It can go without saying that Paul had proven character as he endured those trials. His hope was not found in any earthly treasure.

## HOPE IN CHRIST

What is the result of any affliction in the lives I've talked about, as well as the lives of every Christ-follower? Hope. Hope that is founded in the faithfulness and love of God. We fix our eyes above, on Him that has our life here in His hands at every moment, and most importantly Who has secured our future, for His glory, in eternity with Him. If He proved His love for us as sinners by dying and taking on the penalty for the sin that we deserved to pay for eternally, separated from God in hell, how much confidence ought we to have that He is allowing trials and afflictions only for our good?

As our key passage in Romans 5 continues, we see the reason for our hope defined.

> *⁵and hope does not disappoint, because the love of God has been poured out within our hearts through the Holy Spirit who was given to us.*
>
> *⁶For while we were still helpless, at the right time Christ died for the ungodly.*
>
> *⁷For one will hardly die for a righteous man; though perhaps for the good man someone would dare even to die.*
>
> *⁸But God demonstrates His own love toward us, in that while we were yet sinners, Christ died for us.*
>
> *⁹Much more then, having now been justified by His blood, we shall be saved from the wrath of God through Him.*
>
> *¹⁰For if while we were enemies we were reconciled to God through the death of His Son, much more, having been reconciled, we shall be saved by His life.*

> *[11]And not only this, but we also exult in God though our Lord Jesus Christ, through whom we have now received the reconciliation.*

Dear reader, our experiences, our trials, are the fires that forge the strengthening of our faith. Let us not attempt to pray away the difficulties and adversities God allows us, but rather humbly embrace the circumstances and give thanks to Almighty God, praying that He will cultivate proven character in us as we patiently endure trials and tribulations. Jesus Christ died for us while we were yet sinners, thus enemies with God, saving us from the wrath of God by His shed blood. So, if He reconciled us in that enemy state, how much more assurance does that give us that we will not be forsaken by His love in spite of our afflictions and distresses?

Enduring trials is an experience that helps us identify with Christ and become more like Him. First Peter is a book all about suffering for the sake of righteousness. We are called to humbly submit to God's divine purposes in trials and suffering, knowing that He is ultimately bringing us closer to Him and conforming us to the image of His Son (Philippians 3:10-11).

## Making it Personal

I love when I'm privileged with the opportunity to share with someone how God worked in my life in a circumstance, especially when it can provide practical encouragement if it's similar to their situation. Likewise, I'm encouraged by others sharing their stories of God's faithfulness through their afflictions.

The stories we've looked at in detail are more than likely ones which, by God's grace, we cannot relate to personally on the same scale. These powerful accounts in the faithful believers' lives serve to invoke reverence and awe for God, and to inspire us and convict us of our faith*less*ness in what we go through. They are reminders of the necessity for our humble dependence on our God Most High that knows even the number of hairs on our heads (Matthew 10:30) and is intimately acquainted with all our ways (Psalm 139:3).

At this point, I have only been endeavoring to write this book for two weeks. It has already proven to offer more humbling and convicting enlightenment than I could've imagined! God has been faithful to show me my inadequacy and my desperate need for Him. I started with a very "bare bones" chart that listed all the topics I planned to write about, and each had a few bullet points for specifics underneath.

As much as I am absolutely loving the process of writing, it's far from easy. As I begin each chapter, it can feel very daunting to stare at a blank page. I often don't know how to start or where it's exactly going to go, but God has been faithful to guide me. This experience has given me a tremendous opportunity to recognize my absolute need for Him and my total inadequacy on my own. God is pouring forth opportunity for my enduring patience and character growth, and I'm so grateful. The character development is happening behind the laptop as well as outside my home. Listen to what just happened yesterday...

I completed the writing about Corrie ten Boom and, as you remember, I said that she is the one person from history I'd most delight in having a dialogue with. After concluding yesterday's writing, I joined my husband, Peter, and some of his co-workers for a dinner out.

Three of the young men were new to the company and I had never met them before. The restaurant we ended up at was less than impressive to me. The conversation had been fairly surface and included a bit of discovering things about the newly hired men. As the five men talked about business, I was selfishly rehashing in my mind how less than stellar the food was, and the service even worse. Remember what I just wrote about having a magnifying glass approach, having tunnel-vision in a horizontal approach to any circumstance? Only God could orchestrate this!

Suddenly a lull in conversation provided an opening for one of the young men to surprisingly and "randomly" ask me,

"Sara, if you could sit down with any person from history, who would that be?"

I was flabbergasted at God's providence in the timing of my earlier writing and now the chance to share the ten Boom name with those unfamiliar with the admirable Dutch family. I shared who Corrie ten Boom was and apprised them of the unbelievable timing of the question after writing my book that afternoon.

Despite the providential timing, this also administered a healthy dose of conviction to me in light of what I'd just mentioned learning from the ten Booms' giving thanks to God in everything! How short-sighted and selfish of me to be sitting there bemoaning the quality of food and service, when in the broader picture, beyond the end of my nose, there would arise an opportunity to bring glory to God, and share of the faithfulness and perseverance of one of His saints. Oh, how this still happens far more often than I'd like. We are so utterly hopeless and depraved without Him!

Francis Schaeffer summarized our wretched condition so well in *True Spirituality:*

> The beginning of man's rebellion against God was, and is, the lack of a thankful heart. They did not have proper, thankful hearts – seeing themselves as creatures before their Creator and being bowed not only in their knees, but in their stubborn hearts. The rebellion is a deliberate refusal to be the creature before the Creator, to the extent of being thankful.[5]

We naturally want to be the center of our own universe, and for the world around us to cater to our every desire. One key purpose of the trials God allows in our lives is to sift that prideful, self-centered heart disposition from us, and to cause us to learn a dying to self that can often come no other way than through suffering and trials. In this we are becoming more like our selfless Savior, are we not?

"IF WE SUPREMELY LOVE GOD, WE WILL THANK GOD FOR WHAT HE IS ACCOMPLISHING THROUGH TRIALS. BUT IF WE LOVE OURSELVES MORE THAN GOD, WE WILL QUESTION GOD'S WISDOM AND BECOME UPSET AND BITTER. IF ANYTHING IS DEARER TO US THAN GOD, THEN HE MUST REMOVE IT FOR US TO GROW SPIRITUALLY."
*Pastor John Mac Arthur*

God tests our faith through trials to see who or what we truly love. What we really love in our heart is revealed by how we react to difficulties. Are our eyes fixed on things above or things on Earth? Do we thank Him for what He's accomplishing through each trial and give Him glory?

Trials are valuable for humbling us and weaning us off worldly things. We must avoid the trap of self-pity and instead look outward and upward, expressing gratitude for our divine comfort received, and looking to share the encouragement of that divine comfort in others' lives.

Another reason we go through trials is to subsequently help others in their difficult circumstances. Our unique trials in life, given lovingly by God, ought to enable us to help strengthen and encourage others in their suffering, as God has done for us in our past trials (2 Corinthans 1:3-7). By God's grace, and the Holy Spirit's power, we are comforted and then do the same to help others persevere.

Adoniram Judson served as a 37-year American missionary to Burma in the 1800s. While faithfully living a selfless life to evangelize the Burmese people, Judson was imprisoned, widowed twice, and lost seven children to death. He speaks of God's sovereign ordination in his trials,

*"IF I HAD NOT FELT CERTAIN THAT EVERY ADDITIONAL TRIAL WAS ORDERED BY INFINITE LOVE AND MERCY, I COULD NOT HAVE SURVIVED MY ACCUMULATED SUFFERING."*
*Adoniram Judson*

These lessons may most strongly be driven home through personal experience in the crucible of His testing. But I greatly appreciate when I can glean and implement these life lessons through observation of God's work in others' lives, such as the biblical accounts mentioned previously, or through the lives of faithful saints who have gone before us, such as Corrie ten Boom and Adoniram Judson.

How have you been encouraged by others through esteeming God's faithfulness in their story? That's how we can benefit one another as we simply share life together - conversing about the Lord's providence, and listening to faithful preachers and fellow believers sharing stories of the Lord's faithfulness and kindness in their lives. Tell of His faithfulness, friends.

QUESTIONS FOR REFLECTION
1. In Romans 5:3-5, why does the apostle Paul say we rejoice in our tribulations?

2. In your trials, do you tend to have tunnel-vision on the trial itself? Or how do you keep your eyes lifted to God? Considering a current or recent trial in your life, how could you have lifted your eyes, or if you did, what did God produce faithfully in your life?

3. Looking at the traits of proven godly character listed on pages 21-22, which ones could you begin to pray for God to cultivate in you? Which ones have you seen develop as a result of His trials allowed in your life?

4. Reflecting on others' stories of God's faithfulness in their lives, how have you been most encouraged?

CHAPTER THREE

# FAITHFULNESS IN FEAR
*When I am afraid, I will put my trust in You.*
Psalm 56:3

Fear is the most basic, innate emotion in fallen man, and is a state that likely causes each of us a plethora of issues. In our own power, we will never be completely without fear this side of glory; however, we can find our fears met with comfort or conviction in the scriptures.

Fear to be convicted of is that which is derived from the fear of man, whom we are commanded not to fear in Matthew 10:28. Additionally, Proverbs 29:25 warns, "The fear of man brings a snare, but he who trusts in the LORD will be exalted." While this is a tremendously helpful topic to delve into, one in which the Lord continues to work on in me, this is not the theme of this chapter. Beyond that, there already exists an incredibly biblical and practical book on this subject, which I highly recommend, called *Pleasing People*[1] by Lou Priolo.

Secondly, there is a fear which we all ought to embrace, and that is a godly fear, or reverence for God. Proverbs 9:10 tells us, "The fear of the LORD is the beginning of wisdom, and the knowledge of the Holy One is understanding." Godly fear is a good fear. We are to have reverence and awe for God. My prayer is that this book would invoke some of that reverential fear in you. In 2 Corinthians 7:11, we see how godly sorrow leads to a repentant fear from the realized consequences of sin. Again, another excellent topic to unearth together, but not the aim of this chapter.

Lastly, there is sinful fear that can overtake us in the midst of our circumstances. This might be due to other people, our surroundings and life situations, or quite possibly the fear of not obtaining our perceived needs and desires in any situation. This is the area which we'll dive into in this chapter.

## LESSONS IN THE NIGHT

In 2018 we uprooted from the rolling hills of Tennessee and began to plant new roots in South Florida. On one particular September day, emotions had already been high as I dropped my husband off at the airport for a business trip to Italy - this the 19th day in the home we're renting. Still freshly into this 900-mile relocation, I was missing a familiar life and routine, as well as longing to be establishing our potential forever-home here on Earth, rather than honing my gecko-swatting skills and living out of boxes in a home that would not become our own.

Sleeping had been hit-or-miss for both of us since arriving. I could count on one or two fingers the number of restful nights of sleep I'd gotten so far, and the previous night was no exception. As I laid down to sleep, my mind somewhat racing, replaying details of church conversations just an hour before, and thoughts of my husband's trans-Atlantic flight, I was hyper-aware that it was teeing up to be another restless night.

Though I'd prayed about my sleeping and safety, I still took humanly measures (lights on, etc.) to ward off any imagined intruders. While trying to relax, eye-mask securely in place and sound machine on for noise, I was routinely startled by little pop and crack sounds every so often. My mind would vacillate between an imagined intruder of the human variety and also of the reptile sort. I decided to pull the eye-mask back for a moment to confirm or deny my suspicions at the patio door in front of me.

Fear is not from God (2 Timothy 1:7); therefore, God allowed the enemy of my soul to thoroughly capitalize on this weak moment like never before. I swore that I could see a human outline standing outside the door. I pulled the eye-mask off further to try and verify. My mind and flesh kicked into full-on fearfulness as I grabbed for my bedside flashlight and shone it on the curtain, which was simply hanging there still and innocently. Not yet convinced, I grabbed my bedside handgun and quivered my way over to pull back the curtain.

Much ado about nothing. No one there. Nothing to be alarmed about. (Amusingly, I would realize the next morning that the door handle is on the opposite end of where I was looking anyway!) As I laid back down, thinking it was going to be impossible to sleep, and wondering how I was going to manage the next eight nights of this, the tears started rolling down.

> *"I hate this patio door in my room, I hate the exterior door in the master bathroom, I hate being in this one-story house with geckos, I miss Tennessee, I just want to be in our own new home, I miss being on the second floor..."*

and on it went until God's Spirit broke through the sinful grumbling and clearly spoke Psalm 20:7 to my heart,

> *Some trust in chariots and some in horses,*
> *but we trust in the name of the Lord our*
> *God.*

This isn't even a verse that'd crossed my mind or been in my reading in ages. How gracious is our God to have patience with my fear, with the trust in my "chariots and horses" of lights on and flashlights and guns, and my disregard for the only One who watches over (Psalm 121) and cares about my life more than anyone! The Psalms, especially, are filled with reassurance of God's care for us. He was lovingly, patiently, yet emphatically reminding me that He is my refuge and strength, a very present help in trouble. (Psalm 46:1). We ought to still be responsible citizens to protect ourselves and our loved ones to a reasonable degree, but we must be vigilant to assess where we're putting our trust and hope, and to acknowledge that above all, God is sovereign. No matter what happens, He has allowed every single thing in our lives for our good and His glory.

Not one to mind reinforcement on any lesson, I next appreciated the Holy Spirit's conviction of my misplaced trust, that God could be more sovereign in our former two-story house. Ouch. Truth. I was, again, creating this facade of safety in my mind that I was safe from harm up high. It's really just laughable. God is sovereign over EVERYTHING that comes into our lives. If He is not sovereign, He is not God! As Lamentations 3:37 teaches us,

> *Who is there who speaks and it comes to pass, unless the Lord has commanded it?*

After these two precious and convicting moments of truth, I acknowledged my trust in Him alone and surrendered that imagined control back to Him as well. The immediate peace and rest in my heart carried me off to sleep in only moments. What a blessed encounter with the Living God.

In conclusion to this twilight tale, the second verse of the Gettys' song I mentioned in chapter 2 is very fitting to share with you:

> *Within the night I know Your peace*
> *The breath of God brings strength to me*
> *And new each morning mercy flows*
> *As treasures of the darkness grow*
> *As treasures of the darkness grow.*

Indeed, many treasures of the darkness grew for me through that nighttime trial, and certainly His mercies are new every morning (Lamentations 3:22-23). Praise God!

## ADMONISHING ANXIETY

In Matthew 6:30, Jesus contrasts fear, or worry, to faith. He calls those worried about daily needs "You of little faith!" Sinful fear shows distrust in who God is. It believes the lie that God isn't giving each of us the very best He has ordained for our specific life.

What do you worry about the most? Which worst-case-scenarios do you replay in your mind? Do you worry about your health or your family's well-being? Do you feel anxious that you might never get married or have a baby? Do you feel your stomach in knots when approaching a new situation, a new job, or in having to move to a new city?

The enemy of our souls, Satan, may be targeting each of us in these moments to prey on the fears that most tightly grip us. If he can fuel that fire of lies we're believing, he can get us to sinfully distrust God and doubt God's faithfulness, rendering Him anemic in our minds. It is in these predicaments that we are acting as practical atheists.

I remember the shock value when I first heard the term practical atheism. How could I, as a lifelong believer *in* God and nearly a two-decade follower of Jesus Christ, be dubbed with a term tied to those who don't believe in God? Because I, because we, can live like it.

Self-proclaimed atheists are merely suppressing the truth of God, disregarding Him, since by their denial of Him they are admitting He does exist; if He didn't exist there would be no One to deny. Everyone has the inherent knowledge of God's existence and righteousness, because He put it in each of us (Romans 1:17-21).

Practical atheism creeps in when professing believers make choices that appear to demonstrate they don't believe God exists. External signs, such as church attendance, continue, but further actions and choices paint a different picture as more of a subtle disregard of God creeps in.

How do you live out your faith in pressure-filled moments? What do you do with life-changing news? Do you panic, complain, throw a pity party, start to formulate your own plan of action? Or do you pray, trust God, thank Him for the trial, rest in His sovereignty alone, and follow His leading in His Word? These intense situations reveal our hearts. We can profess with our mouths that we believe in God, but our response to stressful circumstances reveals the level of trust in our hearts.

"ANXIETY COMES WHEN I NEGLECT MY RESPONSIBILITIES TO RELIEVE GOD OF HIS." [2]
*Pastor Mark Mann*

Why is it really that important that we admonish the anxiety we can hold in our hearts? First and foremost, it is dishonoring to God that we're claiming to love, honor, and obey Him, yet we're clearly not doing any of those things by not trusting Him in our actions. Secondly, because an unbelieving world is watching, and how could these enemies of Christ not call into question God's existence when we, as professing believers, are not living as though He does exist! We are living more like Satan than our Savior when our hearts reveal a belief in but rejection of, or distrust in, God (James 2:19).

I exhort each of us holding this book to repent of the ways we live out practical atheism and to turn to God in full trust and obedience in every fearful situation. He is so worthy and capable beyond our comprehension (Jeremiah 32:17; Job 42:2; Matthew 19:26; Mark 10:27; Luke 1:37). Cast all your cares on Him, for He has surpassing greatness in His power (Ephesians 1:19), He is the God of peace and He is faithful (1 Thessalonians 5:23-24), He cares for you as a loving Father (1 Peter 5:7), and He is "near to all who call upon Him" (Psalm 145:18).

## FROM FEARFUL TO FAITHFUL IN SCRIPTURE: MARY

Looking to scripture for some examples of fearful situations that were overcome with faith, let's start with Mary, the servant of God chosen to bring the promised Messiah into this world. As we read in Luke 1:28-38, God sent the angel Gabriel to bring Mary the astounding news.

As Gabriel enters in to greet her and tell her the Lord is with her, verse 29 tells us Mary was very perplexed at the statement and kept pondering what kind of salutation this was. The Greek here for perplexed means "to agitate greatly, to intensely go back-and-forth between inner thoughts and emotions." Mary was apparently fearful, because Gabriel's next statement in verse 30 was, "Do not be afraid, Mary; for you have found favor with God."

We can only begin to imagine the emotions stirring within this young teenage girl's heart, yet the trust she demonstrated during this interaction is awe-inspiring. After the angel reassures her, Mary does not balk at the miraculous news, nor continue on in fear, but she exhibits a steadfastness in the gracious reception of this angelic announcement with a simple logistical question of how the conception will happen since she is a virgin.

Mary's concluding statement back to Gabriel is one that is abundantly fragrant with the aroma of humility in obedience to her Lord, as she replies in Luke 1:38,

> Behold, the bondslave of the Lord; may it be done to me according to your word.

Oh, that we would always take God at His word so quickly and without so many doubts and questions! Mary's obedience is commended through her relative Elizabeth a few verses later in Luke 1:45 when Elizabeth says,

> And blessed is she who believed that there would be a fulfillment of what had been spoken to her by the Lord.

What proceeds from here is an overflow of praise from Mary to her Almighty God – exalting, making great His name, and declaring how blessed she is in His powerful usage of her life. Luke 1:46-55 is also known as The Magnificat, which means "magnify". It is filled with praise to God for who He is and for what He's done and will do throughout generations in the lives of His people.

Mary opens this reverential tribute in Luke 1:46-47 with,

> *My soul exalts the Lord,*
> *And my spirit has rejoiced in God my Savior.*

Mary was mightily and honorably used by God in a most unique way that no one else ever was, nor ever will be. However, it's critical to note that she is also rejoicing in God as *her Savior*. Mary needed a savior just like the rest of us who are sinful human beings, but who come to trust in God our Savior through Jesus Christ, Who saved us, not on the basis of deeds which we have done in righteousness, but according to His mercy (Titus 3:4-7). He is the only sinless, perfect human being that walked this earth, while He was God and man.

Mary's outpouring of praise affirms no greatness in herself, but only the greatness of God alone. She clearly proclaims that God exalts the humble, including herself in that demographic. Mary's example to us is noteworthy, because it is one of short-lived fear and a nearly immediate outpouring of faith, trust, humility, and praise to God.

## From Fearful to Faithful in Scripture: David

The subtitle verse for this chapter on fear is Psalm 56:3. The setting in Psalm 56 is one where David is running for his life as King Saul is pursuing him to kill him. At the point that David pens this psalm, he has ended up in the hands of his greatest enemy, the Philistines. The psalm contains an impassioned contrast back and forth between David's praise and affirmation of his trust in God, and the fact that he is in a distressing situation and is experiencing fearfulness.

It is clear that David did experience fear, so our expectation is not that you and I ought to futilely endeavor to become stoic, impenetrable, steel-hearted, bionic people, but as David freely admits in verse 3, "When I am afraid", then our key implication is found subsequently in verse 4, "I will put my trust in You." We are shown that fear and faith can occupy the same mind at the same moment, but which will be allowed to prevail? Fear without trusting God is sin; John Piper said,

> "Sin is killed by the power of a superior promise."[3]

Faith in God is greater than, thus superior to, fear. David tells us three times in this chapter that it's "In God, whose word I praise" and that in God he has put his trust. David is trusting in God's faithfulness, knowing that God will do what He has said He will do. In this psalm specifically, David is likely trusting God for His promise we read in 1 Samuel 16 that God will give David the kingdom, as He selected him and had him anointed as the next king.

We, too, have God's very word to us in the Bible. The Bible is filled with His revealed will for us, including countless promises to us. Some overarching promises we, as called and blood-bought believers, ought to cling to and rest in when we are afraid, are found in Romans 8:28-39:

- *God causes all things to work together for our good*
- *We're becoming conformed to the image of Jesus*
- *God is for us*
- *It is God who justifies us, and Christ intercedes for us*
- *Nothing will separate us from the love of Christ*

The antidote to sinful fear is the reverent fear of God, and a trust in the Lord Jesus Christ and who He is and what He's done for us. Our hope is based on God's faithfulness, not our current circumstances.

*Let us hold fast the confession of our hope without wavering;*
*for He who promised is faithful.*
HEBREWS 10:23

QUESTIONS FOR REFLECTION

1. What are the three types of fear as described in the opening of this chapter?

2. David is an example to us that fear and faith can occupy the same mind at the same moment. What makes fear sinful? Give scriptural support.

3. What do you worry about the most? How have you handled life-changing news in the past? Why is it really that important that we admonish the anxiety we can hold in our hearts?

4. Read Romans 8:28-39. What are some of the promises God is faithful to fulfill in the life of His people?

## CHAPTER FOUR

# FAITHFULNESS IN UNCERTAINTY

*The steadfast of mind You will keep in perfect peace,
because he trusts in You.* Psalm 26:3

One of the highlights of my childhood was when my dad took me on a trip to California in 5th grade to visit our relatives. It was my first time on a plane, and the weeklong one-on-one time with my dad was cherished tremendously. We vacationed in the San Francisco area, and I remember the excitement and awe of seeing the incredible structure of the Golden Gate Bridge for the first time. Having grown up in northern Wisconsin, in a very small town of less than 1,000 people, the Golden Gate Bridge was remarkable and very out of the ordinary, to say the least.

Though the beautiful, orange vermillion structure and scenic backdrop of the Golden Gate Bridge was impressive to my young eyes, it's what I learned about this architectural accomplishment 20 years later in a Chuck Swindoll sermon that had the most impact. The engineering secret to the massive bridge's durability is that it can sway 20 feet at the center. It is the embodiment of flexibility and strength. Every part of the bridge is related to the two great towers that bear the weight, and the towers are anchored in the bridge's foundation.

Flexibility and foundation are the keys to the Golden Gate Bridge's endurance, and, likewise, these traits are significant in a Christian's life. Our foundation rests on the death and resurrection of Jesus Christ and the numerous promises God has made to us in His word, and this is what ought to give us flexibility, most notably hope, as we navigate life's difficult situations, people, and uncertainties.

## GOING WITHOUT KNOWING

You probably don't have to look further than the tip of your nose to think of someone that has lived through uncertain circumstances in his or her lifetime. We experience even the smallest forms of uncertainty daily, but some of us have been charged with walking an overwhelmingly uncertain path at one time, maybe even more than once, that uprooted us from all that was familiar and comfortable.

Early in the Bible, Abraham paved the way for all believers as an incredible example of a faithful follower who trusted God in the uncertainty of moving. At ages we would deem as senior citizens today, Abram at 75, and his wife, Sarai, were charged with leaving their home and their relatives, and traversing to a destination unbeknownst to them, as described in the account found in Genesis 12-13.

God is pleased with bold faith such as Abraham's, and Abraham is commended for his faith in Hebrews 11:8,

> *By faith Abraham, when he was called, obeyed by going out to a place which he was to receive for an inheritance; and he went out, not knowing where he was going.*

Abram and Sarai knew nothing about any details that lay ahead. Can you imagine relocating from your home and not even knowing at least your destination? For those of us who have moved homes, I think I can assume we all knew which city we were going to! God was faithful to lead Abram to the exact land in which He would bless him and make him into a great nation (Genesis 12:2; 13:15-17)

Abraham's story is far beyond what we can personally identify with. But to some degree or another, have you stepped out in faith, not knowing fundamental details of a pending change, details which may have brought you comfort? How have you been thrust into the arms of the God of all comfort (2 Corinthians 1:3) because He lovingly did not provide all the details for your limited mind to rest in?

## THIS IS MY STORY

God has been pleased to allow my lifelong grip of imagined control to be loosened, and my dependent grip on Him to be tightened, through five moves – which included three states, four cities, and five different bedrooms we've called our own in the course of just over four years. Never did I imagine this would be my story, nor can I any longer claim to have an idea or plan for what is coming next in my life! Thanks be to God, I have learned to close every claim to action with one profound, yet simple, proclamation: "Lord willing"! I will finish this book in 2019, Lord willing. I will see you at church tonight, Lord willing. I will be home for Christmas, Lord willing. *He* orchestrates every detail, not *me*. Not that every spoken sentence needs to end with that phrase, but rather it's about a heart shift. As believers we must repent of a prideful and presumptuous mindset that thinks it knows or can control what's going to happen in our life. We must relinquish our imagined control to the only One in control.

To help you with a high-level visual of our story, in 2014 we sold the house we built and had lived in for over 10 years, and moved into a rented condo only a few miles away in the Green Bay, Wisconsin area. After one year in the condo we moved to the Milwaukee, Wisconsin area so Peter could be closer to his office. We chose to rent there again, because of the belief that it would be short-term and we would possibly have an opportunity to move out-of-state soon. If God willed, we did desire to live somewhere warmer! Just shy of 18 months in Milwaukee, in December 2016, Peter prayerfully took a new job that brought us to Nashville, Tennessee. We loved this move for so many reasons, and I truly believed we were going to retire there. Then, only 20 months after we arrived in Nashville, my husband, again prayerfully, accepted a new role that brought us to the Fort Lauderdale, Florida area, which is where we've been since September 1, 2018.

God has been faithful in His kindness and goodness (Lamentations 3:25) toward me since the inauguration of these southern migrations. For nearly 40 years I lived not much more than an hour from where I grew up. My family is closely knit, and my brother's young kids are an indescribable joy in my life. So moving us gradually and incrementally from having a single- to double- to triple- to quadruple-digit distance between us was an undeserved blessing to this family-oriented heart.

Through all these moves, I had a fitness business, Body and Soul Fitness, that I would start over in each new city. I've always pursued this business as a self-employed, grassroots marketer, relying on God to lead me to teaching opportunities and to grow the business as He saw fit in each area. It's been the biggest blessing to get to know and impact the hundreds of people through the three cities where I've had the privilege to teach.

Before we even left Nashville, I sensed a change in the desires of my heart to continue launching classes in Florida as I'd always done, and my husband even commented once that maybe I could focus on my long-standing dream of writing when we got to Florida.

We left Nashville without our house sold, but ventured south in faith that God would take care of us in His perfect time. Though I'd been fervently house-hunting for two months, when we arrived to Florida we still hadn't found the right home to buy, but, in His kindness, the Lord provided a month-to-month rental house that we were even able to store all our boxes in without needing a storage unit. We rejoiced when we received an asking-price-offer for our Nashville home the night we moved into the rental.

It took seven more weeks to find the home that we ultimately ended up buying. Once we moved in, Peter decided I should I look for a "regular job", so I applied for months and did not get a single interview. I then called a dozen schools and a few community centers to attempt to set up fitness classes, as had been my successful model in the past, but no one took me up on the offer.

Our new home has a separated former office space that was used by the neighborhood developer twenty-five years ago, and one of the first things I thought of was turning it into a studio to host classes right out of my home. I excitedly called the city to ask about the option of having classes in this space, but they swiftly denied that proposition.

One closed door after another led to a bit of discouragement and confusion on my part, and, when one night at church a new friend asked how I was doing and whether there was some way she could pray for me, I answered with transparency. I asked if she would please pray that God's will would be done regarding what I should do with my time living here in Florida – not my husband's will, nor my will, but God's will alone.

One week later, another new friend asked the same question, and I answered the same way. The morning following my second friend's asking, a sponsored ad appeared in my Facebook newsfeed that asked, *"Have you always wanted to write a faith-based book?"* and it was an ad to take part in a free webinar for a self-publishing school. Of course, I registered in excited anticipation!

"KNOWING GOD'S WILL MAY MEAN PUSHING DOWN A NARROW LINE UNTIL YOU HIT A DEAD END. AT THAT POINT, GOD WILL OPEN A DOOR SO WIDE, YOU WON'T BE ABLE TO SEE AROUND IT – ONLY THROUGH IT!"[1]
*Pastor John Mac Arthur*

That morning was the beginning of clarity in discerning God's desire for me at this time in Florida. With Peter in agreement, I began applying what I'd learned in the free webinar that week, and the book theme of God's faithfulness clearly emerged from my mind-map exercise.

As God is able to do far more abundantly beyond all that we ask or think (Ephesians 3:20), we were pleasantly surprised to be able to cut costs in one area of our house remodeling, which allowed us to build in a little desk area for me in that former office space I'd previously asked the city about turning into a studio. I have been so blessed with this dedicated space for writing and having shelves right beside me for all my resource books.

God is so gracious, and He holds every detail of our lives so lovingly in His hands. I cannot urge you strongly enough to cease from the attempt to push through doors that aren't meant to be opened. Let Him lead.

## Unforeseen Blessings

When we step forward in faith, obediently following God's directives in His word to us, we may encounter such unimaginable blessings that would've only been realized under those new circumstances. I can attest to many of these instances that produced spiritual fruit in my life.

God may certainly call some of us to stay planted in one area and work for His glory in that position for a lifetime. But for some of us, He calls us to sow seeds and reap fruit in myriad areas of the world for the length that He appoints each assignment. The opportunity to relocate to new areas brings the opportunity to break away from routine and familiarity, which are sometimes ingredients for stagnancy in our spiritual growth if we are not actively engaging in relationships, education, and situations that bring refinement and sanctification.

By far, the biggest blessing and sanctification tool the Lord has used in my life through all our moves is the opportunity for spiritual growth and sanctification in different church family settings. Sometimes it has been through new resources introduced, sometimes it has been through new opportunities to serve the church body, and sometimes it has been through unique circumstances pertinent to that church body, at that particular time, which brought forth spiritual fruit in only the way the Master Gardener could. He has been faithful to grow and prune me in this season of change.

## Northwoods Bible Fellowship
## Lakewood, WI

We built a cabin in northern Wisconsin a few years before our moves took us out of state. God generously led us to a new church home near the cabin, since we were too far to attend the one where we lived permanently. This is the first time we sat under reformed doctrine expository preaching, and we began to discover the doctrine of election and God's sovereignty for the first time.

We sat under the faithful preaching of Pastor Scott VanLaanen and were challenged through his exceptional expositional preaching. Through Pastor Scott's influence, I learned who world-renowned Pastor John MacArthur is, and thus began a great increase in the caliber of preaching that filled my ears weekly, in the local church as well as through online sermons.

While sitting in Northwoods Bible Fellowship one Sunday, my heart was stirred "out of the blue" to offer up the simple and brief prayer, "God, if you have something for me to do through writing, would you please open that door?" In the fellowship meal following that service, Pastor Scott came over to where Peter and I were sitting and said, "I want to ask you about something." He proceeded to ask if I would be interested in writing our weekly Junior Church lessons for the children. My mind was blown at the immediate, tangible, and personal confirmation that God hears us (Proverbs 15:29), and so very humbled by our pastor's consideration of my service in this vital area. Under Pastor Scott's shepherding and oversight of each lesson, I thoroughly enjoyed my first opportunity of turning an avocation into a voluntary vocation.

Peter and I were blessed to grow, serve, and engage as often as we could with this church body. Peter's baptism as a believer was most certainly a highlight of our time at Northwoods Bible

Fellowship. The Spirit of the Lord is actively working in this church. We were richly blessed with familial relationships built during our 2+ years involvement in this wonderful northern Wisconsin fellowship. This church family also faithfully prayed for us and helped us discern our opportunity to move to Nashville. We are so grateful to continue these precious friendships to this day.

Addendum to the Northwoods era: We lived in Milwaukee during the latter part of our time at Northwoods Bible Fellowship, and, on rare occasions when we didn't go to the cabin for the weekend, we were involved with epikos church in West Allis on Sundays, and also part of a midweek small group in a home. Through the small group, God blessed me with a dear friend who has shown me what a diligent prayer partner looks like, and we continue to lift one another up in prayer still weekly today.

God's hand on our time at epikos was also evidenced by the illumination of my first step toward growth in proper biblical exposition. It was through a church staff friend that God introduced me to expository workshops for women teaching women. I attended a local workshop held at epikos, where we began to learn how to implement techniques for understanding Bible verse context and the author's intent for each passage. This strong desire to learn how to accurately handle the word of God fueled my participation in a workshop of a globally-reaching organization, The Charles Simeon Trust. This was the first of three of their workshops I'd participate in - three weekends where I was humbled greatly, stretched like never before, and saturated with hermeneutical principles (Bible interpretation methods) to exposit scripture more accurately. God was so faithful to continue growing, refining, and educating me in preparation for future service in His name.

GRACE BIBLE FELLOWSHIP
MOUNT JULIET, TENNESSEE
Now knowing what reformed doctrine was, and being firmly locked in on the need to sit under expository preaching, these key words

were the avenue God used to direct our Google inquiry and provide Grace Bible Fellowship as the search result - not only in this web search, but as the answer to where He'd have us integrate into His local church body in middle Tennessee.

Pastor Mark Mann, a fellow Wisconsin native, is shepherding an ever-growing and spiritually-hungry, mature congregation of believers just outside of Nashville. God knew that this church would become home rather instantaneously to this Midwestern girl's heart.

The depth of teaching and supplementary studying that goes on at Grace Bible Fellowship was second to none in my Christian experience. The prevalence of a biblical counseling mindset is palpable and is woven through nearly every conversation with Pastor Mark and among seasoned church members. Biblical truths and mankind's timeless heart conditions are exposed and explored deeply as a close-knit, small church family numerous times per week.

The Lord was pleased to bring us to Grace Bible Fellowship during the time that, after 10 years of renting, these faithful saints would become owners of their first church building. We were richly blessed to work shoulder-to-shoulder with our church family in the demolition of parts of the existing structure, and then to enjoyably pitch in and perspire through various construction tasks to finish off the long-anticipated, beautiful new worship space.

I consider Grace Bible Fellowship as a "sanctification central" of sorts in my 20 years of walking with the Lord. God mightily used theologically-rich book after book alongside the dynamic expository preaching of Pastor Mark, coupled with his skillful counseling in the private ministry of the Word, to increase my understanding of proper doctrine, to grow me in Christlike character, and to refine and prune off habitually sinful patterns to which I was spiritually-blind for decades.

In our time at Grace Bible Fellowship, by God's grace, I grew in numerous ways. I solidified my finite, humanly grasp on God's sovereignty, recognized His two-fold will as described in scripture, saw the power of biblical counseling over integrated secular

49

counseling, discovered the richness of the Puritans' writings, learned more deeply about dying to and fearing myself, and truly embraced the profoundly imperative mindset which concludes every claim to action with the submissive and obedient words, "Lord willing" (James 4:13-15). What occurred in only 19 months with this church was a gift from the all-knowing, only wise, always good, merciful, and gracious hand of our loving Heavenly Father.

## TRUST THROUGH THE UNKNOWN

Needless to say, it was never a quick, easy, nor straightforward decision to move on from either of these homes/churches and embrace the unknown yet again. So many dear people were covering us in prayer each time, and I ultimately trusted in God's sovereignty and my husband's leadership through God's defined marital structure in Ephesians 5:22-24, as He allowed these moves for our good and His glory.

> *God is our refuge and strength, a very present help in trouble. Therefore we will not fear, though the earth should change...Be still and know that I am God.*
> PSALM 46: 1-2, 10

God has been abundantly generous and kind to lead us directly through the doors of another dynamic, theologically-sound, and uncompromising diverse body of believers here in South Florida at Grace Bible Church Plantation. We were welcomed with open arms by our new church family members from day one, and we have been hearing preaching through the pages of scripture that has deepened our biblical understanding and corrected some lifelong errant insights in various areas of scripture. God has been lavish in aligning much of the semi-weekly preaching with what I've been writing about at that exact moment in this book. I am overwhelmed by His love and kindness. We are also thankful for the opportunities we've had to serve, and for the faithful shepherding we're under, which God is using to challenge and strengthen us in doctrinal maturity and conformation to Christlike character.

I would absolutely not be where I am today without the sequential path God sovereignly and lovingly ordained through these multi-state moves. My trust in Him has grown exponentially and He has refined me every step of the way. God's word is full of many truths for how we can trust Him and how He is sovereign, but I also find comfort in these wise words penned by Charles Spurgeon,

"HAD ANY OTHER CONDITION BEEN BETTER FOR YOU THAN THE ONE IN WHICH YOU ARE, DIVINE LOVE WOULD HAVE PUT YOU THERE."[1]
*Charles H. Spurgeon*

How do we process and navigate and find hope through so much change? Through faith by His grace. Hebrews 11:1 tells us,

> *"Now faith is the assurance of things hoped for, the conviction of things not seen."*

Verse 6 of the same chapter affirms that

> *"without faith it is impossible to please Him for he who comes to God must believe that He is and that He is a rewarder of those who seek Him."*

## WHAT WE KNOW IN THE UNKNOWN

When the desired roadmap appears blank, and the direction of our future seems unclear, where can we always find the assurance of foundational truth and seek rest in the only wise Cartographer's guidance – solely in God's precious word to us.

> "Lift up your eyes on high and see Who has created these stars, The One who leads forth their host by

number, He calls them all by name; because of the greatness of His might and the strength of His power, not one of them is missing."
ISAIAH 20:26

"He is before all things, and in Him all things hold together."
COLOSSIANS 1:17

"The One forming light and creating darkness, causing well-being and creating calamity; I am the Lord who does all these." ISAIAH 45:7

"Many are the afflictions of the righteous, but the LORD delivers him out of them all." PSALM 34:19
"Both riches and honor come from You, and You rule over all, and in Your hand is power and might; and it lies in Your hand to make great and to strengthen everyone."
1 CHRONICLES 29:12

"And my God will supply all your needs according to His riches in glory in Christ Jesus."
PHILIPPIANS 4:19

"Do not fear, for I am with you; do not anxiously look about you, for I am your God. I will strengthen you, surely I will help you, surely I will uphold you with My righteous right hand."
ISAIAH 41:10

"He gives strength to the weary, and to him who lacks might He increases power."
ISAIAH 40:29

²⁹Are not two sparrows sold for a cent? And yet not one of them will fall to the ground apart from your Father. ³⁰But the very hairs of your head are all numbered. ³¹So do not fear; you are more valuable than many sparrows."
MATTHEW 10:29-31

"Now He who supplies seed to the sower and bread for food will supply and multiply your seed for sowing and increase the harvest of your righteousness"
2 CORINTHIANS 9:10

"And He is the radiance of His glory and the exact representation of His nature, and upholds all things by the word of His power. When He had made purification of sins, He sat down at the right hand of the Majesty on high"
HEBREWS 1:3

"also we have obtained an inheritance, having been predestined according to His purpose who works all things after the counsel of His will"
EPHESIANS 1:11

"The mind of man plans his way, but the Lord directs his steps."
PROVERBS 16:9

## BRIDGING THE CONNECTION
In closing, is it now clearer how a Christian's life ought to resemble the reasons for the Golden Gate Bridge's endurance over nearly a century? Foundation is our why, and flexibility in our circumstances is our how. We do not find security because of our circumstances, but because of faith in Who has ordained our circumstances and Who

is unchanging no matter how volatile and variable our life's path may appear.

We don't find rest or unrest *because* of our circumstances or level of certainty, but we rest *in* all circumstances because of *God's power and sovereignty*. He is the One who holds all things together and works all things for our good, if we love Him and are called by Him (Romans 8:28).

## QUESTIONS FOR REFLECTION

1. Think of a time of uncertainty in your life. How did God give you flexibility, specifically hope, and strength when He did not provide all the details for your limited mind to rest in?

2. Consider a current situation that is filled with uncertainty or unknowns for you. Which verse in the section *What we Know in the Unknown* most ministered to your heart (or choose your own) and why? Offer God a prayer of thanksgiving describing how you can trust Him in this.

3. Write out Hebrews 11:6.

4. What does it mean to find rest in circumstances versus finding rest because of circumstances?

## Chapter Five

# Faithfulness in Our Sin, Discipline, & Growth

*All discipline for the moment seems not to be joyful, but sorrowful;
yet to those who have been trained by it, afterwards it yields the
peaceful fruit of righteousness.*
Hebrews 12:11

We would've been blessed to have parents that allowed trials to complete their work in our lives and to actively engage in the discipline necessary for each disobedient situation. Blessed are the children whose parents discipline them and do not deny them the pain of suffering consequences of their sin. To do so is to help grow and mature the child, as well as to model God's pattern that though there is forgiveness, He can allow consequences of our sinful actions (Galatians 6:7).

I admire the tenacity of parents that immediately address their children's foolish and sinful ways in the moment the heart is revealed for what it is. Several of my friends are incredibly diligent and skilled at addressing when their children are not acting in a God-honoring way; for example, pointing out a behavior in the moment to help their children understand their lack of self-control in a situation, or their failure to consider others before themselves. Discipline in our lives, beginning at a young age and continuing until death, is for our good and is given by God for our sanctifying growth and holy refinement.

The highlighted verse with this chapter's title is Hebrews 12:11. After the first ten chapters of Hebrews define God the Son as our King and Priest, chapters 11 and 12 give us the response of faith. Earlier in Hebrews 12, the author is cross-referencing Job 5:17, Proverbs 3:11-12, Psalm 119:75, and Revelation 3:19 when he says,

> and have you forgotten the exhortation which is addressed to you as sons, "My son, do not regard lightly the discipline of the Lord, for those whom the Lord loves He disciplines, and He scourges every son whom He receives.
> HEBREWS 12:5-6

The author goes on to inform the reader how God deals with us as His children, because who as a responsible parent doesn't discipline his or her children. Subsequently, if God is not disciplining you, you are not His child (Hebrews 12:7-9). The author of Hebrews explains God's purpose behind disciplining us in verse 10 - God disciplines us for our good, so that we may share His holiness, the purity of His character.

## THE FRUIT OF DISCIPLINE

I mentioned some of God's attributes in chapter 1, which included attributes that we cannot share with Him (omnipresence, immutability, sovereignty, etc.), but He also has characteristics that we ought to desire to share, to be sanctified toward a better reflection of His image, which brings Him glory. These character traits are what can be developed through our trials in His loving discipline - traits such as holiness, lovingkindness, goodness, justness, mercifulness, graciousness, faithfulness, patience, truthfulness, and possessing wisdom.

We can have assurance and trust in God's purpose for our discipline, because He assures us of the beneficial reason for it and it is not for punishment. The reality of punishment was already done on the cross!

Discipline leads to restoration. For instance, when I'm straying in a way that's disobedient to God's commands, wrestling with an uneasiness while living life according to the desires of my flesh in some way, my Merciful Father lovingly brings discipline into my life to reveal my sinful heart and convict me of my sin so I seek His forgiveness. He restores me into my restful, peace-giving, and secure relationship with Him. Discipline produces short-term pain for long-term gain.

> "ALL TRIALS ARE FOR TWO PURPOSES: THAT WE MAY BE BETTER-ACQUAINTED WITH OUR OWN WICKED HEARTS, AND THAT WE MAY BE BETTER ACQUAINTED WITH OUR OWN BELOVED SAVIOR."
> *George Whitefield*

To further build the point that our discipline purifies our character, by taking a look back to Deuteronomy 8:1-6, we can clearly see that God allows our trials so we can see what's in our heart and test whether we remain obedient to Him during His test. Our trials, our disciplines from Him, are nothing short of loving mercies from a patient and kind Father who only has our best in mind.

Do you accept discipline of the Lord gladly? Proverbs 3:11-12 says,

> *My son, do not reject the discipline of the LORD or loathe His reproof, for whom the LORD loves He reproves, even as a father corrects the son in whom he delights.*

Likewise, Psalm 119:75 states,

> *I know, O LORD, that Your judgments are righteous, and that in faithfulness You have afflicted me.*

How is it that God even bothers with us - do you ever ponder that question? I've thought that innumerable times. Most often the question is born out of a perspective-shaping, immense gratitude following my vitally valuable time in His refining crucible. When I see Almighty God's patience in my sin-filled life, I wonder why He even "gives me the time of day"! It is so profoundly humbling to consider, and it ought to keep us appropriately low in the accurate view of ourselves.

> "THERE IS NOTHING DESTROYED BY SANCTIFICATION BUT
> THAT WHICH WOULD DESTROY US."
> *William Jenkyn*

Those God has chosen before the foundations of the world (Ephesians 1:4) belong to Him, and therefore He loves us with a jealousy that is for our good. He loves us too much to allow us to settle for less than His best; therefore, trials, afflictions, and discipline occur in varying frequencies in a believer's life.

## ADMIRING A JEALOUS GOD

Have you ever sung a song for years and, when you really stopped to think about it, not truly known or understood the meaning of the lyrics? I'd sung "How He Loves", written by John Mark McMillan and made known by David Crowder Band, for nine years before even scratching the surface of understanding the powerful depths professed in the truth of these lyrics.

"He is jealous for me." Not until later years in my walk with the Lord did I truly understand how God is jealous for us (Exodus 20:5). This is not jealousy as we commonly understand it. He is not jealous because He wants something He doesn't have; everything and everyone are already His (Psalm 24:1). He is jealous when He sees us worshiping anything else above Him. Worship, praise, and adoration belong to Him alone, as only He is worthy. He is jealous for us in the sense that He knows we will not be completely satisfied with

59

anything or anyone besides Him, and He wants us to find that fulfillment in Him alone (Jeremiah 2:13).

A line in this song, "How He Loves", that I sang rather mindlessly all these years is, "When all of a sudden, I am unaware of these afflictions eclipsed by glory…"[1] That's a bit of a lyrical mouthful, isn't it? These lyrics were somewhat imperceptible to me until I experienced God's foreknown afflictions through discipline in my life, embraced His sovereignty in all things, and saw His glory eclipse my humanity.

"AND I REALIZE(D) JUST HOW BEAUTIFUL YOU ARE, AND HOW GREAT YOUR AFFECTIONS ARE FOR ME. OH, HOW HE LOVES US…"[1]

Psalm 119:71 says, "It is good for me that I was afflicted, that I may learn Your statutes."  In the moment of any affliction or discipline from the Lord, we may immediately believe life is not supposed to be this way. Or we may have a difficult time imagining getting to the other side of the situation. As the psalmist states, we learn God's statues when we're afflicted, and we can even look back and say it was good. God's afflictions draw us back into obedience to His word.

> *Before I was afflicted I went astray, but now I keep your word.*
> PSALM 119:67

Likewise, Job 36:15 tells us that in affliction is when God opens our ears. Maybe you can look back and recognize how you repeatedly ignored God's warnings and opportunities to get your attention prior to the affliction, yet you hardened your heart to His Word and charged forward with your own agenda to please yourself and not Him.

"GOD WHISPERS TO US IN OUR PLEASURES, SPEAKS IN OUR CONSCIENCE, BUT SHOUTS IN OUR PAIN: IT IS HIS MEGAPHONE TO ROUSE A DEAF WORLD."
*C.S. Lewis*

Discipline can bring myriad lessons. I've learned a lot about covetousness and contentment. Did you know that covetousness is at the root of every sin? As we've touched on previously, if we are not genuinely thankful in our heart to God in all circumstances (1 Thessalonians 5:18) it ought to be acknowledged as rebellion against God, a lack of trust in Him, and essentially the belief that He's not enough or He doesn't know our needs best.

A lack of contentment follows closely on the heels of covetousness. When everything seems to be going our own way and we are loving life, deceptively "content" in every way imaginable, have you considered that this is actually a form of discontent? What if several of those aspects of your so-called-content life were instantly taken from you? Would you continue to thank God and find equal contentment? The fact is that we often proclaim contentedness because of circumstances or possessions or relationships. But if any of those were removed, perhaps by the aforementioned afflictions, would we find ourselves in a state of discontent? Or is our Creator God, our Heavenly Father that has loved, called, redeemed, and restored us to Himself for eternity, more than enough for us in this and every moment? That is a good litmus test for each of us. Do you trust God no matter the afflictions and discipline He allows on your journey? Do you call these trials good, because He is good? Everything God does is done to display His glory, majesty, and goodness, and, when involving discipline, can also refine and transform us into His likeness.

"AFFLICTIONS ARE AS NAILS, DRIVEN BY THE HAND OF GRACE, WHICH CRUCIFY US TO THE WORLD. AFFLICTIONS ARE THEN BLESSINGS TO US WHEN WE CAN BLESS GOD FOR AFFLICTIONS; WHOSE SINGLE VIEW IN CAUSING US TO PASS THROUGH THE FIRE, IS ONLY TO SEPARATE THE SIN HE HATES FROM THE SOUL HE LOVES."
*Augustus Toplady*

I absolutely love the above quote by Augustus Toplady. It is such a powerful reminder to me when disciplinary circumstances lovingly ordained by God have awakened conviction and necessary pain in my life, because they are drawing me closer to Him and further from the sin that ensnares me.

## OBEDIENT AND PROACTIVE GROWTH

It would not be beneficial to conclude this chapter on discipline and jeopardize you believing that our main avenue of growth in Christlikeness comes only through discipline and trials. God uses pain when necessary to lead us to the cross, but by His grace alone this may not be a daily circumstance. Spiritual growth ought to occur daily through consistently feasting on the transformational truth found in God's word alone.

We are obedient to God's word if we strive for living a godly, spotless life by faith in and dependence upon Christ. We are not striving for holiness in an effort to earn eternity in heaven, as that clearly contradicts scripture (Romans 6:23, 10:9-10, 11:6; Ephesians 2:8-9; Titus 3:5), but we are living out our faith in obedience and unparalleled gratitude for our transformational, saving faith given by God alone. As commanded in 1 Timothy 4:7, "discipline yourself for the purpose of godliness." We ought to be diligent to pursue godly virtues, ongoing repentance, faith, and obedience to the Word. This is only accomplished by God's grace.

Pursuing spiritual growth is imperative for the redeemed. Despite prevalent and popular heretical teaching in this world, we are not saved to then rest on our laurels and enjoy sinful worldly pleasures, following every desire of our flesh, because God in Christ has covered our sin with His shed blood so we can enjoy life to our own pleasing. This is called antinomianism. As Paul warns believers in Romans 2:4-8,

> *⁴Or do you think lightly of the riches of His kindness and tolerance and patience, not knowing that the kindness of God leads you to repentance? ⁵But because of your stubbornness and unrepentant heart you are storing up wrath for yourself in the day of wrath and revelation of the righteous judgment of God, ⁶who will render to each person according to his deeds: ⁷to those who by perseverance in doing good seek for glory and honor and immortality, eternal life; ⁸but to those who are selfishly ambitious and do not obey the truth, but obey unrighteousness, wrath and indignation.*

God's word commands us in the second half of 2 Peter 3:14, "be diligent to be found by Him in peace, spotless and blameless". Take very seriously your faith, and grow in a greater knowledge of who God is (2 Peter 3:18). Pursue becoming more like Christ. Relentlessly remove anything hindering your spiritual growth. Live in light of the truths you learn on the treasured pages of scripture. Thank God for every loving display of His merciful discipline, and for His Spirit-led strides of sanctification exhibited in your life, and live life to bring glory to His name.

1. Why does God discipline His children, and what traits can be cultivated through His loving discipline of us?

2. According to Proverbs 3:11-12, whom does God discipline?

3. Read Psalm 119:71. Why is it good that He afflicts us?

4. Reread the quote by Augustus Toplady on page 62. Prayerfully ask God to search your heart to discover if there are any past afflictions for which you have not recognized God's sovereign refinement as a blessing in your life.

5. Discipline is one way God grows us, but to proactively grow in Christlikeness we must take very seriously our faith, and grow in a greater knowledge of who God is. In what ways are you in regular pursuit of becoming more like Christ?

After prayerful consideration, what might God want you to remove from your life that is hindering your spiritual growth?

## Chapter Six

# Faithfulness in Disappointment
*The mind of man plans his way,*
*but the LORD directs his steps.*
Proverbs 16:9

If I could ask you when the last time was that you were disappointed, I wouldn't be surprised to hear that it was already from something that happened (or didn't happen) today, or at a minimum something from this past week. Why do we experience disappointment? Why do we continue to set ourselves up for disappointment?

As I learned from Pastor Mark Mann, "inflexible expectations are preplanned disappointments." Going deeper to the root of these inflexible expectations, though, why do we presume to know what's best for us or even set our sights on outcomes without consulting God and His Word to discern His will first? A short but powerful five letters that goes back to the Garden of Eden and our original parents' sin: P R I D E.

Pride in a person's heart, and we all have plenty of it, thinks it knows what's best, even better than God's best, for one's life. We may pridefully map out a life plan for the long-term, as well as a plan for each day's activities and tasks, but Who is ultimately in charge of that map? Being a good steward of our time and making the most of our days (Ephesians 5:16) is a worthwhile and relevant mindset to embrace, but to paraphrase our key verse in this chapter's opening, despite the plans we have in mind, the LORD directs our steps.

Disappointment reveals our true heart. Our reaction to anything reveals what's important to us, what we worship, and how we're not trusting God. We'd be wise to use these regular opportunities to examine our heart before God and, in repentance, ask for His help to grow in our trust of and submission to Him.

> "HUMAN HISTORY IS THE LONG TERRIBLE STORY OF MAN
> TRYING TO FIND SOMETHING OTHER THAN GOD WHICH
> WILL MAKE HIM HAPPY."
> *C.S. Lewis*

## DISAPPOINTMENTS AS TESTS

As I sit writing this chapter, the Lord was faithful to give me some unexpected material this week to write about regarding an initially disappointing circumstance I experienced. I'm writing from a reclining chair, because it's too uncomfortable for my back to sit in a desk chair. Last Saturday I ran a 5K after only running one other time in the past 12 months. I was surprised to run the whole the 5K without walking, and this fueled my past passion for running and participating in events again. I began eagerly looking into upcoming events and recruiting friends to participate. I even found another local 5K this coming Saturday while a friend is visiting from Chicago, and we made plans to run it.

Two days ago, which was two days after the 5K, my low back locked up. As I reached down to pick something up, a familiar, sharp, seizing pain radiated through my low back. This is far from something new. It most severely occurred in 2006 and had me immobile with a back brace for a good week, and since then has been an occasional occurrence that has always left me disappointed, because of the forced slow-down of my daily life and the alteration of planned activities during that time.

Knowing what I know now about God's sovereignty and His allowing of things only for our good, I slowed my mental pace this week and examined my heart motives in the sudden eagerness to get back into running and events. There is purpose in our pain; therefore, God has allowed this low back issue to manifest itself in His perfect timing.

66

As I sought Him and examined my heart, I could genuinely admit that my desire for running was for vanity reasons and pride in my (perceived) own abilities. Running itself is not actually that enjoyable of an activity for me, nor am I even gifted at it, but it keeps weight off like nothing else. The fact that I could accomplish the 5K without stopping fueled my vain desire to drop some pounds, and it also ignited an intention to pursue a past passion which had proven to feed a competitive and self-focused spirit within me. I'm already selfish enough without having an unspiritual distraction to pull me away from my God-ordained focus on my home and growing in Him (Titus 2:3-5), to alternatively be pouring effort into something that feeds worldly values of appearances (1 Samuel 16:7). I'm not implying exercise is inherently bad, because we ought to endeavor to take care of our bodies (1 Timothy 4:8), but what fills the heart behind the motivation to do or not do something is what reveals idolatrous or impure motives, and this is imperative to examine when our hearts feel pulled strongly toward something outside of disciplines of the Lord.

> *for bodily discipline is only of little profit, but godliness is profitable for all things, since it holds promise for the present life and also for the life to come.*
> 1 TIMOTHY 4:8

Disappointments happen on so many levels. Young children throw temper tantrums over not getting a treat at the store, or for not being given the particular plate they want to use for dinner – things that seems so ridiculous to us as adult. But, in some cases, we can act no differently. I've seen grown men get into very heated verbal arguments at the airport check-in counter over who was truly next in line! People berate restaurant servers and management over a disappointment in the food they were served. We routinely hear people express disappointment over the weather! Our selfish hearts demand perfection, immediate gratification, and our way right away. Why do we get so worked up over such trivial, earthly things? We think they will provide happiness and satisfaction to our hungry hearts.

> "MAN IS ALWAYS SEEKING FOR WHAT HE CAN NEVER FIND – SATISFACTION IN EARTHLY THINGS. HE TOILS AFTER HIS OBJECT, AND WHEN HE HAS GRASPED IT, HE TOILS STILL; THE POSSESSOR OF ABUNDANCE, NOT OF HAPPINESS."
> *Charles Bridges*

## DISAPPOINTMENT IN DESIRES

I can assure you that I have been, and continue to be more often than I'd like, disappointed in things such as restaurant food preparation, weather, and daily, trivial inconveniences. But at a deeper level, I have also shed many tears in the past from a deep heartache over the disappointment of God's withheld blessing (Psalm 127:3) of having a baby.

I married a man who'd already had three children in a previous marriage. He was transparent from the first week we met that he'd had a vasectomy. At that point the information really rolled right off me, and, being optimistic by nature, I assumed a reversal surgery would work just fine someday.

After getting married and having an immediate family with three children 50% of the time, I went through a phase where I didn't have the desire to even add a baby to the mix. Four years into marriage, the maternal stirrings I'd had from a young age began moving in my heart, and we discussed Peter having a vasectomy reversal.

God saved me after college, but He'd given me His heart for the value of family long before that. I vividly remember the time in a college class where we were asked to write a statement about where we saw ourselves 10 years from that point. As the class shared aloud their answers, one by one the responses of the young, career-driven students all had a similar echo to each other regarding positions in organizations achieved or salary amounts earned. With a stark contrast, I proudly stated my goal to be, "successfully raising a happy and healthy family."

So, it came as no surprise to me that my heart was again stirred to desire having my own children after marriage. In 2004, Peter graciously underwent the painful vasectomy reversal surgery for 6 hours. It was a rough recovery and much more difficult to endure than the original surgery. In the months following, I was rather consumed with doing all I could to time the best opportunity for achieving a pregnancy. Peter also did many selfless things to try and help the situation medically on his part. Month after month there was a letdown and disappointment. Months turned into years.

In 2006, there was a painfully pinnacle moment that crushed my heart like nothing before. My friend also married a man with the same situation, and after a few years of marriage they decided to have his reversal surgery done as well. My selfish assumption was that they'd end up with the same results as we did, and at least misery loves company, right? My friend's husband had a very painless surgery and recovery, and then only one month later I got the call that brought me to my knees. My friend called to share their exciting news that God had blessed them with a pregnancy already. It took all I had within me to hold it together on that brief phone call and share in her excitement, as I was trying to politely end the call as soon as possible before I burst into tears out of my own pain and deep disappointment for my life. I remember falling into Peter's chest with the news, but now I can reflect with gratitude that the Lord was kind to have the call come when I had the loving support of my husband to lean on in that very moment.

I don't recall the exact details of my frame of mind on a monthly basis after that, but I know that it was still top-of-mind to have a baby, and baby showers were another painful occurrence time-after-time. Additionally, until you've walked this path, you have no idea that Mother's Day in church can actually feel like one of the most awful days of the year when the deep ache of the desire for a child goes unfulfilled year after year. And in some churches it's all flowers and celebration without regard to this being an extremely difficult day for many, for various agonizing reasons, in the pews. I am grateful for our last few churches that have kept their Lord's Day focus on Who it ought to be on 52 weeks of the year.

My consumption and heartbreak over this long-lived desire of my heart definitely lessened as the years passed, but in 2014 God was ever-so-faithful to deliver me from this idol of my heart that I continued to covet in discontentment. While at a conference on my birthday weekend, April 12, 2014, the Holy Spirit pierced through my heart in such a freeing way, and released me of the grip that had held my heart and mind for over 10 years, when Matthew 10:37 was spoken,

> He who loves father or mother more than Me is not worthy of Me; and he who loves son or daughter more than Me is not worthy of Me.

This verse is in the context of Jesus instructing His disciples on what a true disciple will look like. He is teaching them not to fear man when testifying of Him (Matthew 10:17-31), and that families will be split because of those who follow Christ and those who oppose Him (Matthew 10:34-38).

Matthew 10:37, which pierced to the depths of my marrow (Hebrews 4:12), is implying that one who truly loves and follows Christ has a love for even his own family members that so pales in comparison to his love for Christ that it can be deemed hate. Love for Christ ought to be so great that one would be willing to forsake family ties (in my application, desire of children) for His sake if they were detrimental to obedience in following Christ wholeheartedly. Pastor John MacArthur declares, "the true disciple fears not the world, favors the Lord, forsakes the family, and follows the call."[1]

I promptly wrote alongside this verse in my Bible, "His will, not mine, for a baby." I was convicted in my unbelief that God was not all-wise in knowing what was best for me, and convicted likewise that I was presuming to know best what I needed. I had allowed my single-focused devotion that ought to be on Him to be lowered to grasping for fulfillment on earth. Oh, for grace to trust Him more!

Do not mistake that I'm saying that a desire for children is a bad thing or that forsaking your family for no reason is a good thing – the crux of the issue is whether you are allowing something in your heart to be more important than your love for and obedience to God. If you are worshiping something or someone above God, then it is idolatry to you.

I'm also not implying that everyone who has an unfulfilled desire for children is idolatrous in that desire. I'm saying that any unfulfilled desire that becomes an *ultimate* desire in your heart can be causing you to sin. This happens by staying so fixated on a desire that it consumes you to the point of worshipping that desire over worshipping the one true God and submitting to His will for your life no matter the cost. If that describes your degree of disappointment, then that is an idolatrous desire. Covetousness is sinful, and discontentment is distrusting God's sovereignty, having unbelief in His perfect will for your life. He alone is perfect and good and sees the picture of our whole life in its entirety. As the hymn *Day by Day* declares, "He, Whose heart is kind beyond all measure, gives unto each day what He deems best, lovingly it's part of pain and pleasure mingling toil with peace and rest."[2] Friend, there is so much peace when we release our grip on the idols of our heart.

## Thy Will be Done

An interesting thing has happened since moving to Florida. As I mentioned, since April 12, 2014, that idolatrous grip for having a baby was released in a moment, and I have felt free and content in the Lord's plan for my life ever since. We are now part of a rather young congregation at our church in Florida, and I have been privileged to watch my new friends skillfully and wisely parenting their young ones like no one else I've seen before. Many of these mothers also homeschool their children, and I see the value in these methods firsthand. Having a front-row-seat to these somewhat unfamiliar approaches to child-rearing have gently stirred that old, familiar desire in my heart to cherish an opportunity to mother the same way. The crucial, colossal difference that I'm experiencing now, though, is that it's a desire I fully and immediately release to the Lord for His will alone to be done. His will was always done before, and always will be, but obedience is found in the complete and total surrendering of my heart and spirit, which is the key difference now. I can survey the lives that my friends are living here and think, "That might still be pretty neat to do, too", yet in the next breath freely and wholeheartedly say, "but Thy will be done."

Handling disappointments is not a matter of asking God to take away the desire or to fulfill the desire, rather it's about learning to long for the best desire.

*Because Your lovingkindness is better than life, my lips will praise You. So I will bless You as long as I live; I will lift up my hands in Your name. My soul is satisfied as with marrow and fatness, and my mouth offers praises with joyful lips.*
PSALM 63:3-5

1. What do disappointments reveal about us?

2. What is the difference between having a healthy desire in your heart and having an idolatrous desire?

3. When considering deep disappointments in your life, prayerfully ask God to search your heart to discern whether there is an idol that your heart is gripping onto. Record what He reveals and/or write a prayer to Him confessing any sin He reveals and asking for help in these areas.

4. Find and list scripture references to support the truth that longing for God is our best desire.

## CHAPTER SEVEN

# FAITHFULNESS IN LOSS

*And He has said to me, "My grace is sufficient for you,
for power is perfected in weakness."*
2 Corinthians 12:9

"I could never imagine going through that!"
"I would never have been able to handle that!"

These are statements I've heard from people of all ages for over 25 years now, and, truthfully, I'd probably have said the same thing to them in the past if the life circumstances were reversed. I don't think we can ever comprehend how loss will affect us specifically until we experience it firsthand.

People have made the claim that "God won't give you more than you can handle." And in one sense, this is true. When Christians are tempted to sin, God is faithful to not allow believers to be tempted beyond what they can handle. He will always provide a way of escape (1 Corinthians 10:13). But in another sense, Christians can never handle life's temptations and difficult circumstances in their own strength and power (2 Corinthians 12:9). In life's circumstances in general, if we were able to handle everything in this fallen world ourselves then why would we have a need for God? It is absolutely His strength, His power, His sovereignty, His grace, His mercy, and His love that sustains us through all of life's sometimes exciting, sometimes excruciating, but always dynamic seasons. We must trust in Him alone, lean hard into Him for strength and comfort, learn to grow from His appointed afflictions, and drink deeply from his infinite wellspring of love.

## DADDY'S GIRL

I am the oldest of my parents' two children, and the only girl. To describe my dad as delighted and overjoyed to have his first child arrive on April 12, 1976 is still a highly diluted description of his paternal pride! My dad was as exuberant as they come, and he was suited to be a father more than anyone I'd known growing up. Named Sara, which means princess, my dad naturally called me this nickname, and I embraced the title and the unique place in his heart.

Not that I can remember it firsthand, but I was my dad's sidekick on many adventures as a baby and toddler. He took me along every Saturday morning to run errands around town, always concluding with a stop at the local bakery to get cookies. Though I cannot recall the specific memories from such a young age, these shared experiences with my dad undoubtedly established and cultivated the sense of love and security that I knew throughout our relationship.

My dad worked professionally for the Boy Scouts, and, when it wasn't too improper, I even got to tag along for some short meetings. This continued as he moved into outside sales jobs in my childhood, and, in the summer, I would occasionally ride along with him all over the state for his sales calls.

We have pictures of me up under the hood of my dad's truck "helping" him fix the engine – I even had my own little matching tiny screwdriver for the job. Saturday morning home projects like that would often lead to taking a garbage run to the dump (I lived in the country – in the city you'd probably say a landfill!). Of course, I rode along for the trips to the dump! Fly-fishing, bow-hunting, you name it, I was alongside my dad no matter what he was doing.

We were, and still are, incredibly blessed to own a home on a beautiful, clear lake in northern Wisconsin. Summer afternoons, for my brother and me, were spent in anticipation of our dad getting home from work so we could immediately jump in the lake and have him pull us waterskiing behind the old 18HP outboard motor fishing boat. Life was simple, but sensational.

I was about 12 years old when my dad underwent triple bypass open heart surgery. He was generally a healthy man by all appearances, and he was extremely health-conscious in trying to control his blood pressure and cholesterol, but he had genetic factors that contributed greatly to his health struggles. Before he underwent this invasive, major surgery, my dad recorded cassette tapes for both my brother and me. They were tapes to be given to us on our 13th birthdays regardless of the outcome of the heart surgery. God graciously saw my dad through this bypass surgery, and life continued on as normal.

I became a typical teenager that didn't think her parents were necessarily all that exciting anymore, but no matter what age I advanced to, my dad was always a safe place to turn when I wanted to talk about anything. My dad fostered this net of security for me at a young age in, ironically, a hammock hanging between two towering oaks atop the hill in our backyard by the lake. He encouraged me to ask him for a "hammock talk" whenever something was on my mind that I needed to talk about. Oftentimes, he could "read me" and sensed that something was awry, so he initiated the hammock talk between us. My dad was a remarkable example of our Heavenly Father's love and care for us as His children. Additionally, in gratitude for the depth of my dad's character, meaningful one-on-one conversations are still one of my favorite ways to spend time with people.

The other constant through my childhood and into older years was the love of thunderstorms my dad inspired in me. When the cracks of thunder and flashes of lighting filled the dark sky in the middle of the night, my dad would come see if I was awake, or maybe even wake me up, to see if I'd like to join him from the safety of our porch to marvel at God's power on display in nature. My dad wanted to teach me to not fear the storms, but it also generated incredibly cherished memories that I hold dear in my heart to this day.

## LIFE REDEFINED

On a cold Friday night in my senior year of high school, October 22, 1993, our ordinary, small-town lives, and the lens through which I look at life, would change forever. It was time for the weekly high school football game, and, as a member of the drill team for that semester, I was chosen to carry the American flag at the start of the football game. My US Army veteran, and at that time Army Reserve, father chose to endure the cold, autumn temperatures so he could see me take up the Stars and Stripes, but my brother was sick, and my mom stayed home with him in the cold weather.

After a normal first half in the student section with my friends, and then participating in the halftime show with the band, I stopped to briefly talk to my dad on my way back from the field. He was standing alongside the fence by the track with many other men watching the game. I remember my dad asking me if I had any money on me for hot chocolate. I said I didn't and that I was going home since it was too cold, then I went on my way. That's about all I remember from that conversation.

I listened to the remainder of the football game on the radio at home with my mom and brother. We live about 10 minutes or less from the football field, so when 15 minutes had passed after the game ended, we became only slightly perplexed as to why dad wasn't home yet, but we quickly excused the situation with the fact that he was extremely social and was more than likely caught up talking to someone after the game.

When about 30 minutes had passed, we started to understandably get concerned that maybe something was wrong. This was in the days before cell phones and instant communication options were ubiquitous. Then the phone rang. My mom took the call from a friend who had to wait until arriving back at her home to even make the call. The message details were scant but concerning. "Jim was having numbness on his face and arm at the football game and was taken away by ambulance." This friend relayed to my mom that my dad's last words to her while going to the ambulance were to let his family know not to worry.

The nearest hospital to us is 30 minutes away. My mom became obviously concerned and felt unable to drive, so I was willing to relieve her of the burden. I remember thinking, in my naïve and "invincible" 17-year-old mind, that this was probably not anything too major, and maybe a "false alarm" heart situation that we'd be bringing my dad home from later that evening. So, having already been ready for bed, I put only one contact lens back in, just having enough vision to get by and save myself some time later.

The three of us headed toward the city with the hospital and met up with the ambulance intercept near the city limits. A better-equipped ambulance had been dispatched, and met up with the original ambulance along its route. We parked on the side of the road in front of the two ambulances, and my mom got out to go see what she could find out, not allowing us to go see for ourselves. She came back with no more answers than we already had, except that my dad was unconscious already, so it was going to be a matter of waiting for tests to be performed to get some answers.

As we trailed the ambulance to the hospital and parked near the ER door, the sight of my dad being taken out of the back of the ambulance seated on a gurney is etched as clearly in my mind as what I just saw on my plate at lunch today. The level of concern elevated in my heart at that point.

The next hour or two determined that my dad had had a massive stroke, a brain aneurysm had burst in the center of his brain at a point that was believed to be inoperable due to the extensive damage that would occur in getting to it. We then had him transported to a more specialized hospital facility in Green Bay in the hope that they could still do something with a shunt to preserve his life.

As we drove to Green Bay, I imagine we were each praying desperately, crying out to God for miraculous help. Though I was raised in a church, and freely admitted to belief in God from a young age, I did not have a saving relationship through Jesus Christ until I was 22 years old. The details of my faith through this tumultuous event with my dad are very vague, as faith was not the central focus of my life as it is now.

At the Green Bay hospital, we waited through the night with family members and friends joining us, but it was apparent there was nothing that anyone could do to save my dad's life. By late Saturday morning I watched the life of my beloved father vacate his earthly body and pass from this life onto the next.

## A NEW NORMAL

What I remember through the intense grief and deep feelings of loss in the weeks and months that followed my dad's death was the outpouring of support from family and friends, and the reassuring belief that God was with us and was still in control. I can't even express how thankful I am that God allowed my heart to remain soft and receptive to Him through an event that often hardens many in their intense hurt, anger, and confusion. I did not have a clear understanding of a saving and regenerating faith at that time, but God was sustaining my heart in a steadfast trust in Him despite the profound hurt and confusion I felt.

We made it one day at a time, and God gave my mom strength to continue forward in our, now, family of three. He provided abundant support through loving friends to meet needs in practical ways and to counsel her. My mom felt reassured of God's love and presence through truths the Holy Spirit brought to mind to dispel her fears and give her hope at one of her lowest and loneliest points in the weeks following my dad's death. God was her refuge and strength, a very present help in this time of need (Psalm 46:1).

My mom made the choice to become better instead of bitter from this loss. God continues to be faithful to use my mom to bring beauty from ashes in the ways He has allowed her to help many new widows in their moments of overwhelming grief. She has redeemed the loss she's experienced and learned to be present for others in their storms. I've seen the fulfillment of truth found in 2 Corinthians 1:3-4,

> *Blessed be the God and Father of our Lord Jesus Christ, the Father of mercies and God of all comfort, who comforts us in all our affliction so that we will be able to comfort those who are in any affliction with the comfort with which we ourselves are comforted by God.*

My mom was widowed a second time 17 years later, but she has still maintained an unwavering trust in and reliance on God, as she has written, "I cherish my memories and will carry them with me forever as I move forward embracing life and the beautiful gifts God provides for us each day. I am grateful to have been given a second, and now third, chance at life and love, and I embrace the future knowing God has promised to be with me always."

## QUESTIONING GOD

I think it comes rather naturally for all of us as finite, fallen humans to inquire "Why?" of God when unforeseen events take place. Life may completely change in an instant or, oftentimes, circumstances simply don't go as we thought they should or would. Asking God the question "Why?" is an occurrence with believers we also see in scripture (Joshua 7:7; Psalms 10:1, 74:1, 88:14). We question God, because we cannot perceive what He is doing. We are, however, called to trust God in humility and contentment, resting in the hope found only in Him. We sometimes have to *choose* to trust, circumnavigating whatever our feelings may be, and believe God for who He is and what He's promised.

We would be wise to ask God in faith for a humble heart and childlike trust, as modeled by David in Psalm 131. David writes that he does not involve himself "in great matters, or in things too difficult" for him. Things too difficult and too marvelous for us refers to knowledge that belongs to the Lord alone, things we are not privy to understand (Psalm 115:3; Isaiah 55:8-9). As Deuteronomy 29:29 states, "The secret things belong to the LORD our God", and these things are His purposes decreed before creation. Our restless, relentless, and impatient questioning of God reveals the pride in our hearts that is elevating our will above God's.

God is never caught off guard, He is never surprised, He is never blind-sided, He is never frustrated by something He didn't see coming. There are no "what ifs" or "if onlys" with God. "As for God, His way is blameless" (Psalm 18:30). He is not simply responding to what we do; He's proactive, not reactive. That is something I never understood for decades of my life.

*Oh, the depth of the riches both of the wisdom and knowledge of God! How unsearchable are His judgments and unfathomable His ways!*
ROMANS 11:33

Trusting God's sovereignty over every meticulous detail of our lives is imperative as believers. In addition to the primary truths I implore you to discover in the Bible, *Trusting God*[2] by Jerry Bridges is a book I'd love to see in the hands of every new (and seasoned) believer. Bridges clearly conveys a wealth of understanding he gleaned from his lengthy Bible study on the topic of God's sovereignty during his own time of adversity.

## LESSONS THROUGH GRIEF

After God saved me in 1998, I was able to start looking back at all that happened in the loss of my dad and recognize His provision and His kindness in ways I hadn't seen before. He was our Provider and Protector, as He always was and will be. I experienced His unfathomable love and grace before I'd even turned to Him fully.

In the key verse (2 Corinthians 12:9) mentioned under this chapter's title, the apostle Paul was receiving a response from God in regard to Paul's plea for his painful hindrance to be removed. God would not remove this thorn, but He would continually provide the grace Paul needed to endure the affliction. God's grace shines forth from our weaknesses. I love how the original text in the Greek reads, "I will rather gladly boast in my weaknesses, that the power of Christ may overshadow me." In a world striving for the spotlight, how beautiful it is to rest in the shadow of the Almighty (Psalm 91:1). I know I wrote a lot of detail about my dad's life and death in this chapter, but what I pray you take away from this book is the recognition of the overshadowing power that Christ has been at all times in my life – through joy and especially through sorrow.

> "GOD TAKES AWAY THE WORLD, THAT THE HEART MAY
> CLEAVE MORE TO HIM IN SINCERITY."
> *Thomas Watson*

In a felt loss of this magnitude, one aspect that changed my life is the way I look at time on earth as fleeting. Our true home, as believers, is not here, but our time here on Earth is "just a vapor that appears for a little while and then vanishes away." (James 4:14), and we are to make the most of it for God's glory. I've seen the truth from Ecclesiastes 7:2 echoed throughout my life since October 22, 1993,

> *It is better to go to a house of mourning than to go to a house of feasting, because that is the end of every man, and the living takes it to heart.*

82

Because I've known so well how lives can be gone in an instant from this world, I've endeavored to prioritize my time here to be used meaningfully and to build into relationships that are important. The above verse implies that when we experience deaths, or adversities, we are deeply reminded of what's important, and our priorities are rearranged in our heart. We certainly gain and grow more in character through trials than pleasures. My dad taught me not to fear storms, and my Heavenly Father teaches the same truths about life. Likewise, Charles Spurgeon said, "Fear not the storm, it brings healing in its wings, and when Jesus is with you in the vessel the tempest only hastens the ship to its desired haven."

I am grateful God allowed me to learn this lesson at a young age. I'm not implying that I was happy to lose my dad at age 17 - by no means - but I have accepted this life-changing incident as good, because I know God is only good, and He is loving and merciful; He is wise and His ways are higher than my ways (Isaiah 55:9). This is part of the life story God has allowed me to steward for His glory. It's a thread within the perfect, unique, lifelong tapestry He's weaving of His daughter named Sara, and I pray that I live it out in a way that's pleasing to Him.

"WHEN PEACE, LIKE A RIVER, ATTENDETH MY WAY,
WHEN SORROWS LIKE SEA BILLOWS ROLL;
WHATEVER MY LOT,
THOU HAST TAUGHT ME TO SAY,
IT IS WELL, IT IS WELL WITH MY SOUL."[3]
*Horatio G. Spafford*

1. Refute the familiar statement, "God won't give you more than you can handle."

2. Read 2 Corinthians 1:3-4. What does God do for us in our loss (any affliction) and how does He then use us to help others?

3. As Solomon describes in Ecclesiastes 7:2, the living take it to heart when faced with others' deaths. In what ways has God reframed your perspective and beliefs through deaths?

4. Write out Isaiah 55:9. Ask God to search your heart to discern whether there are any areas of loss where you may be sinfully resentful toward Him despite His sovereignty in all your circumstances. Record your results.

## Chapter Eight

# Faithfulness in Salvation

*If we say that we have no sin, we are deceiving ourselves and the truth is not in us. If we confess our sins, He is faithful and righteous to forgive us our sins and to cleanse us from all unrighteousness.*
1 John 1:8-9

My extended family was blessed to have the beautiful presence of a most joy-filled, godly matriarch among us for 86 years, my great aunt Edith. I treasure the fact that I have possession of her tattered and time-worn, pages-falling-out, electrical-tape-bound Word of God. My great aunt, whom I regretfully didn't take the time to get to know well enough in the height of my self-focused adolescence, is a testimony to God's faithfulness to keep her persevering through trials and holding unwaveringly to her faith.

From what I can ascertain, my great aunt Edith and great uncle Henry got married as unbelievers. My great aunt was called by God into saving faith not too far into their marriage. Her Bible margin notes, and family members' accounts, tell me that Auntie Edith endured some difficult times for decades in their marriage when Uncle Henry drank alcohol and spoke unkindly. I also see clear, documented evidence of God's strength and Spirit-filled joy in her life amidst these trials. Uncle Henry was most definitely an enjoyable and gregarious character of a man, by all worldly standards, but drinking alcohol altered his behavior to be mean-spirited, at times.

Fast-forwarding many decades, God took my Auntie Edith's life peacefully in September 2007 after she had matured to age 86. Her funeral was such a wonderful and powerful celebration of her earthly life devoted to God and for her eternal homegoing to heaven.

She and Uncle Henry had both been residents at an assisted living facility in her last days, and Uncle Henry continued living there. On Christmas Day 2007, only months after his lifelong love of over 65 years was gone, we went to visit Uncle Henry. The dialogue that had taken place prior to us heading for the door to leave is inconsequential. What happened in the final moments of our visit was of eternal significance.

As we were wrapping up the conversation and starting to indicate we were ready to leave, my great uncle began speaking in somewhat of a mumble saying, "I've never been a churchy person...that was Edith's thing...", so we all leaned in to determine what he was talking about. He continued on, repeating with obvious concern, that he was not a "churchy person" and he'd done so many ashamed things in his life.

My stepdad, Fred, who was a pastor the last twelve years of his life, carried a deep and loud enough voice that Uncle Henry's dull ears could engage. Fred began sharing the gospel with Uncle Henry and conveying the truth that it didn't matter what he'd done in the past, that he could call out to God with a repentant heart, trusting in Christ for salvation, to be washed clean from his sins, and he wasn't required to earn this - that the free gift of God is eternal life in Christ Jesus our Lord (Romans 6:23).

Uncle Henry confirmed that he indeed wanted to surrender to Jesus Christ as his Lord and Savior, and with tears streaming down all our faces, Fred prayed with Uncle Henry, and a six-decade-long prayer of my Auntie Edith was answered through God's salvation, we believe, of her lifelong love.

When one comes to saving faith in Christ, a call and a faith given by God alone, repentance, confession, and submission to Christ are necessary heart-changes that God effects in a new believer's life. No man can read another's heart, but the joy-filled change that was visibly evident in my great uncle's demeanor for the remaining three weeks of his life would lead us to believe we witnessed the true, effectual call of God to save Henry's life.

## GOOD NEWS

My great uncle's testimony of life lived as a believer was a brief, albeit powerful one. God is faithful to save those He has chosen before the foundation of the world (Ephesians 1:3-5); maybe when they're 9, maybe when they're 92 and weeks away from dying, only God knows.

I grew up in a church that God used to foster my belief in Him and to learn some practical tools such as memorizing the books of the Bible in song format. I did not hear the gospel message except when I went to Bible camp in 2nd grade. I responded to that general calling by raising my hand to "accept Jesus", because who could listen to a talk on heaven and hell as a child and then willfully choose hell? That day was a memory I have, but not an effectual call of God on my life that resulted in repentance, confession, and submission to Christ as Lord, resulting in conversion and conformation to His Word. It was a stepping stone along the path of my faith.

I may have thought I chose heaven that day, but the truth is God does the choosing. We're the ones that need acceptance by Him! God did truly draw my heart at age 22, and then my eyes were opened to a new, saving faith that I had definitely not known in my life before.

By and large, we all think that heaven is our default destination. Have you ever been to a funeral that it was *not* implied that the deceased was now "in a better place" or "reunited with loved ones"? I haven't. I grew up with that common belief that pretty much everyone goes to heaven when they die, except maybe the really bad guys who do terrible crimes or openly reject God.

You know what the immense irony is here? *We* truly *are* the bad guys, too (Romans 3:10, 23; Isaiah 53:6 Psalm 14:1-3; 1 John 1:8,10). Romans 3:10 says, "There is none righteous, not even one." Without Christ we have no ability to stand righteous before God, and we will all stand before Him one day to give an account for our life (Romans 14:10).

God created a perfect world in the beginning. As our Creator, He has authority over all the world; everything is His (Psalm 24:1). Sin's introduction to the world began in the Garden of Eden through Adam and Eve's Fall when tempted by Satan. As a consequence of the Fall, all of mankind is born morally corrupt, enslaved to sin, at enmity with God, and unable to please Him or turn to Christ for salvation on our own.

God is holy (Leviticus 11:44-45; 1 Peter 1:15-16). He is perfect and without sin, and because of that He has a holy standard. Matthew 5:48 declares, "Therefore you are to be perfect, as your heavenly Father is perfect." God hates sin, and sinners can never stand (be approved) in His presence (Psalm 1:5). But one day we will all stand before the judgment seat of God (Romans 14:10-12; Revelation 20:13-15).

An attribute so often glossed over in many churches today is the fact that God is just. He created us and we are accountable to Him. He is perfect and we are not, therefore in that natural, fallen state of sinfulness, where would that leave us with a just God? The severe future reality is described in 2 Thessalonians 1:8-9, that when Jesus returns to Earth He will be:

> *dealing out retribution to those who do not know God and to those who do not obey the gospel of our Lord Jesus. These will pay the penalty of eternal destruction, away from the presence of the Lord and from the glory of His power*

This all creates a perilous predicament for us as sinful, imperfect humans. In my naïveté decades ago, I thought that if I could master my behaviors, I could live a life without sin. Naïve or not, that's such a preposterous and ludicrous idea, because actions are only one way in which we sin. The genesis of all sin begins in the heart – meaning the inward place of our affections and desires.

Heart-level sins are prolific – I couldn't even name them all here. Think about the last time you felt jealousy or envy for something someone else has. Have you been bitter over someone's success that you coveted for yourself? Maybe you can recall the dishonoring or unloving word spoken to your spouse this morning. You may have looked at someone yesterday with lust in your heart. Perhaps an item rang up lower at the store than the shelf price listed, and you considered it a win for yourself instead of speaking truth. Have you lied to anyone this week, even a little twist of the truth to cast yourself in a more favorable light? Basically, if we're breathing, we're sinning.

As Romans 3:23 tells us, "for all have sinned and fall short of the glory of God", and all means everyone that's ever been on this planet from the precious newborn (Psalm 51:5; John 3:6) to pastors, priests, and the pope, to the sweetest elderly lady you know at church, to everyone but Jesus documented in the Bible. "There is none righteous, not even one", states Romans 3:10.

With the plethora of religions in the world, or even considering people who are living life free from any ties to a church or organized religion, the question remains for each living soul, what do you do about your sin?

In our helpless state we can do nothing to earn our salvation (Galatians 2:16). Romans 3:20 states, "because by the works of the Law no flesh will be justified in His sight". There's nothing we can do to work our way to God, to earn a place in heaven, to help outweigh the bad with good, to give enough money or say enough of the right prayers. No amount of good works, nor the keeping of God's laws, can be sufficient to atone for sin.

*But* there is good news, which is what the word *gospel* means. The best news ever is that God made a way for our us in our helpless, sinful state to be able to stand in His spotless, holy presence. God became man; this is the reason we celebrate Christmas. Fully God, fully man, the Lord Jesus Christ lived a pure and sinless life on Earth (1 John 3:5; 1 Peter 2:22, Hebrews 4:15). Jesus

Christ became the sacrifice for our sins on a cross. He took God's wrath upon Himself and shed His blood as our atonement, and the way of salvation was provided. God raised His Son up from the grave as proof that He had accepted Jesus' sacrifice, and believers would be justified – made right legally – with God (Romans 3:21-26, 4:25). As Romans 3:24 states, we are "justified as a gift by His grace through the redemption which is in Christ Jesus". The uncomplicated, unparalleled, and unfathomable message of forgiveness for those otherwise deemed for hell is found in 2 Corinthians 5:21,

> *He made Him who knew no sin to be sin on our behalf, so that we might become the righteousness of God in Him.*

It literally took my breath away one day when I felt the weight of the truth of that scripture, which means that when God sees us, as redeemed and reconciled believers, He sees Christ's pure and spotless righteousness that covers us, not our filthy sinfulness. God the Father treated Christ as a sinner on the cross, though He was not ever a sinner, and Christ died in our place to pay the penalty for the sins of those who believe in Him.

Jesus Christ is alive; He rose from the grave three days after His crucifixion. He conquered death and sin and Satan, and that is why we celebrate Resurrection Sunday, or Easter. As a child my favorite holiday was undoubtedly Christmas, because of all the new toys I'd get as gifts. As a believer, my favorite holiday has undeniably been Easter for the past two decades, as I exuberantly rejoice in the greatest gift I've ever received – forgiveness, reconciliation, and eternal life from my Heavenly Father. Truthfully, every day feels like Easter when you acknowledge the gospel every day and praise God for it!

## COUNTING THE COST

For those who respond to this free gift of salvation through the Lord Jesus Christ, God asks us to respond in repentance and faith, trusting and submitting to Jesus Christ as Lord and Savior (Acts 17:30, 26:20). Repentance in the Greek means "change the mind."

> ## "REPENTANCE IS AN INWARD MATTER, WHICH HAS ITS SEAT IN THE HEART AND SOUL, BUT AFTERWARDS YIELDS ITS FRUITS IN A CHANGE OF LIFE."[1]
> *John Calvin*

The way in which the Bible commands repentance is not a once-and-done occasion at the moment of salvation, it's a lifelong crusade in which one routinely recognizes and confesses sin to God, and, by God's grace and in His strength, repents and turns to go the opposite way from that sin. Our lives ought to look markedly different year after year from the way our lives looked in the past (2 Corinthians 5:17). God has given us a new heart and put a new spirit in us (Ezekiel 36:26), so it is imperative that our lives look differently than before we surrendered to Him. Truly repentant believers will lapse into sin occasionally for the rest of their lives, but they will always find their way back on the narrow way, thanks be to God.

Jesus talked about this narrow way in Matthew 7:13-14.

> *"Enter through the narrow gate; for the gate is wide and the way is broad that leads to destruction, and there are many who enter through it.*
>
> *For the gate is small and the way is narrow that leads to life, and there are few who find it."*

This vital verity ties back to what I mentioned earlier in this chapter about the fact that by and large, as a society, we think that heaven is everyone's default destination. These powerful two verses completely refute that unfounded logic. The Lord Jesus Christ Himself stated that the way is broad that leads to destruction, or hell, and there are many who enter through it. That is a severely sobering thought. Jesus said there are few that find the way that leads to life.

Wide and broad versus narrow and few. Two gates, two ways, two destinations, two groups of people. We're looking at two ways that two categories of people are believing they will find eternal life with God. Wide and broad does not solely mean those who openly reject God; it would include all religions that are works-based and teeming with self-righteousness to "earn" your eternal life. These religions are not declaring one single and definite way to eternity with God - works-based religions such as Roman Catholicism, Mormonism, Jehovah's Witnesses, Hinduism, Buddhism, Islam, and Christian Science are examples of broad road religions.

An equally harrowing series of verses articulate the fact that not everyone, particularly in the context of churches, will spend eternity with God. In Matthew 7:21-23, Jesus says, "'Not everyone who says to Me, Lord, Lord, will enter the kingdom of heaven...And then I will declare to them, 'I never knew you; depart from Me, you who practice lawlessness.'"

Jesus continually affirmed the difficulty of following Him because it requires denial of self and enduring persecution from the world (Matthew 10:38, 16:24-25; John 15:18-19, 16:1-3), and it allows for only one route to salvation. As Acts 4:12 states, "And there is salvation in no one else; for there is no other name under heaven that has been given among men by which we must be saved." This makes for a narrow gate and road, which few find.

Salvation is by grace alone, through faith alone, in Christ alone (Ephesians 2:8-9; Romans 3:28; Titus 3:4-5), but it is not an easy road. The life of a Christ-follower calls for knowledge of the truth, repentance, submission to Christ as Lord, and a willingness to obey His will and Word. Our life as a believer is no longer our own, we have been bought with a price (1 Corinthians 6:19-20).

I HAVE BEEN CRUCIFIED WITH CHRIST; AND IT IS NO LONGER I WHO LIVE, BUT CHRIST LIVES IN ME; AND THE LIFE WHICH I NOW LIVE IN THE FLESH I LIVE BY FAITH IN THE SON OF GOD, WHO LOVED ME AND GAVE HIMSELF UP FOR ME.

*Galatians 2:20*

The truth that our life is no longer our own is a compelling reminder for professing believers, and is a realistic cost to consider for those who have not come into saving faith in our Lord Jesus Christ. Paul Washer states this transformation so well:

> *To put it simply, the Christian now loves the God he once hated and hates the self he once loved; he now desires the righteousness he once spurned and despises the unrighteousness of which he once boasted.[2] Prior to regeneration and conversion, the sinner is a lover of self and pleasure, and a hater of God and good (2 Timothy 3:2-4). However, in the titanic work of conversion, God regenerates or recreates the heart after His likeness in true righteousness and holiness (Ephesians 4:24)[3]. A new convert will not only have a new relationship with God and His people, but also an altered relationship with sin and the world. He will be averse to the sin he once loved and contrary to the world in whose path he once walked.[4]*

If you have not truly understood the gospel until today, or never rightly responded to the gospel, or you recognize that there hasn't been genuine fruit from your faith or repentance exhibited in your life, then if you sense God working in your heart right now, I urge you to place your faith in Christ alone today, bowing your knee to His lordship over your life. Come to Him in faith alone, trusting that

He has done the full and complete work to save you from your sins. He will continue to help you remove sin from your life from this day forward, so you will bring Him glory and others will see these good works and praise His name (Matthew 5:16). If this is truly God's work happening in your heart, then you can be assured that you'll begin experiencing a change of mind and a growing faith as you pursue righteousness and find a new and fulfilling pleasure in walking daily with your Creator.

## QUESTIONS FOR REFLECTION

1. If you are a blood-bought believer in the Lord Jesus Christ, in what ways do you see how He's been faithful to grow you in becoming more like Him? What looks different in your life than at the time He drew your heart in salvation?

2. Read Galatians 2:20. What are the implications of this verse in your life and how have they been evidenced?

3. Read Romans 14:10-12. Who will give an account to God?
Read Matthew 7:21-23. Is everyone that claims to know God going to enter heaven? Why?

4. Read Ephesians 2:8-9 and Titus 3:4-5. What are the components of saving faith mentioned in each verse?

# FLAWED GIRL, FAITHFUL GOD

*Tell of His glory among the nations,*
*His wonderful deeds among all peoples.*
Psalm 96:3

Thank you. Thank you, dear reader, for using your finite time to read this book, and for being open and curious to learn about some of the numerous ways that the God of the universe has shown Himself faithful through the eyes of this jar of clay (2 Corinthians 4:7). My desire is that this book has lifted your eyes higher to behold our great God with more reverence, in greater awe, through increased trust, filled with unceasing hope.

When Peter and I got married July 1, 2000, some dear friends gave us an oval wooden plaque that still hangs on our wall today. It has carved in it three profound, yet simple, words: "God is Faithful". Still being somewhat young in my saving faith at the time, though I was thankful for the gift, I could not have explained what that powerful three-word statement truly meant. To be a writing a book 19 years later, centered on the premise of that succinct statement, is such a strong testament to the transforming power of God's work in my life. He has proven Himself faithful every single time to see me through refining trials individually and as a couple. To God be all glory!

For the endless list of God's gracious acts in my life, proclaiming His kindness, goodness, and faithfulness to others is the least I can do. This ought to be our aim as believers. We don't all have to write books about God's faithfulness in our lives, but more than likely we all come into contact with someone every day. Take those opportunities to encourage someone with how God is working in your life, or how you see Him working in theirs. Use social media for God's glory and to make Him known. Take the time to speak truth, and love and serve others.  As we read in Hebrews 10:24, "and let us consider how to stimulate one another to love and good deeds."

This quote from Alexander MacLaren inspires me and captures my heart behind the passion to write this book:

THE NATURAL RESULT OF BEING FILLED WITH GOD'S SPIRIT IS UTTERANCE OF THE GREAT TRUTHS OF CHRIST'S GOSPEL. AS SURELY AS LIGHT RADIATES, AS SURELY AS ANY DEEP EMOTION DEMANDS EXPRESSION, SO CERTAINLY WILL A SOUL FILLED WITH THE SPIRIT BE FORCED TO BREAK INTO SPEECH. IF PROFESSING CHRISTIANS HAVE NEVER KNOWN THE IMPULSE TO TELL OF THE CHRIST WHOM THEY HAVE FOUND, THEIR RELIGION MUST BE VERY SHALLOW AND IMPERFECT. IF THEIR SPIRITS ARE FULL, THEY WILL OVERFLOW IN SPEECH.
*Alexander MacLaren*[1]

It's been my joy and privilege to pour out to you records of God's faithfulness and grace through these pages. If you know Him, I exhort you to go and do likewise, proclaiming God's name and giving Him glory throughout the whole world.

# Notes

## Introduction
1. Quoted from Keith Getty at *Sing! 2018* conference and noted by Rusty Benson, AFA Journal https://afajournal.org/past-issues/2018/december/sing/

## Chapter One
1. Thomas Chisholm, *"Great is Thy Faithfulness"*, 1923
2. Matt Stanchek, *"We Must Put on the Character Qualities of Christ that Serve to Foster Unity in the Body"*, gbcplantation.org, 3/31/19

## Chapter Two
1. Keith and Kristyn Getty, *"When Trials Come"*, 2005
2. W.E. Vine, Merrill F. Unger & William White, Jr., *Vine's Complete Expository Dictionary of Old and New Testament Words*, 1996
3. Matthew Henry, *Matthew Henry Commentary on the Whole Bible (Complete)*, 1706
4. Corrie ten Boom, *The Hiding Place,* 1971
5. Francis Schaeffer, *True Spirituality,* 1971, 2011

## Chapter Three
1. Lou Priolo, *Pleasing People,* 2007
2. Mark Mann, *"The Ascension of Jesus Christ"*, https://www.sermonaudio.com/sermoninfo.asp?m=t&s=56 19146102505, 5/5/19
3. John Piper, *Desiring God,* 1986, 2011

## CHAPTER FOUR
1. John MacArthur, *Found: God's Will* p.59
2. Charles H. Spurgeon, *Morning & Evening: Evening Devo*, November 11, 2019 www.heartlight.org/spurgeon/1111-pm.html

## CHAPTER FIVE
1. John Mark McMillan, *How He Loves Us,* November 29, 2005

## CHAPTER SIX
1. John MacArthur, *The Hallmarks of Discipleship, Part 3,* August 30, 1981 https://www.gty.org/library/sermons-library/2284/the-hallmarks-of-discipleship-part-3
2. Lina Sandell, *"Day by Day"*, 1865

## CHAPTER SEVEN
1. Charles H. Spurgeon, *"Ziklag; Or, David Encouraging Himself in God"*; MTP 27, Sermon 1606, p. 373
2. Bridges, Jerry, *Trusting God*, 1988, 2008
3. Horatio G. Spafford, *It is Well with My Soul,* 1873

## CHAPTER EIGHT
1. John Calvin, *Commentary on a Harmony of the Evangelists, Matthew, Mark, and Luke Đ Volume I*, 1555, 2015
2. Paul Washer (@paulwasher). As quoted in chapter. 5/31/19, 9:47 AM. Tweet.
3. Paul Washer (@paulwasher). As quoted in chapter. 5/28/19, 4:34 PM. Tweet.
4. Paul Washer (@paulwasher). As quoted in chapter. 5/24/19, 1:04 PM. Tweet

## CONCLUSION

1. Alexander MacLaren, *Alexander MacLaren's Expositions of Holy Scripture* (quoted from Acts 2 commentary), 2013

Made in the USA
Columbia, SC
04 August 2019